AND NOW A WORD

And Now a Word from Our Creator

Thomas G. Savage, S.J.

LOYOLA UNIVERSITY PRESS
Chicago   60657

LIBRARY OF CONGRESS
CATALOGING IN PUBLICATION DATA

Savage, Thomas G., 1926-
  And now a word from our Creator.

  1. Universities and colleges—Sermons.
2. Catholic Church—Sermons.   3. Sermons, American.   I. Title.

BX1756.Z8S28   252'.02   72-1370

ISBN 0-8294-0213-6

Photos from
Photographs│Algimantas Kezys, S.J.
Loyola University Press, 1966

CONTENTS

Preface, xiii

Apology, xvii

PART I

JESUS, THE CHRISTIAN,
AND THE WORLD

And now a word from our Creator, 3
Jesus didn't know polyglas
    from poligrip, 11
Jesus: good shepherd or good guru? 19
Jesus never sang
    "The Star-Spangled Banner," 25
The importance of being ethnic, 32
Holden Caulfield and Jesus:
    catchers in the rye? 38
Jesus and ecology, 45
Not the rap, but the map, 49
Not the man, but the plan, 57

vii

PART II

THE CHRISTIAN:
HIS FAITH AND HIS CHURCH

Led by the Spirit, 63
The undergraduate and mystery, 70
Believing is seeing, 75
Faith and certitude, 81
Thinking with the church, 86
My church has an unlisted number, 92
The Christian ritualist, 99
Worship: giving and receiving, 104
Up against the wall, mother church, 111
If you're out of the church,
    you're out of fear, 117

PART III

CHRISTIAN HOPE, LOVE,
AND CHARITY

Man's trust in God, 125
What, me worry? 129
God in the technological age, 137
Taste was no problem at Pentecost, 143
Required for graduation:
    intelligent love, 149
Love and self-deception, 155
Christian self-denial and charity, 160
Charity and functional living, 165
Love and self-interest, 170

PART IV

FOR CHRISTIANS: MORALITY AND
A LIFE OF PRAYER

Confusion is our middle name, 177
The spirit of God and
   the good life, 184
Man's moral attitude, 188
Christian conscience today, 193
The intellectual and morality, 200
Happy are they who read, 208
Personal prayer and
   social awareness, 215
Prayer puts it together, 220
Man's status, 228
Daily bread or daily surrealism? 232
The impromptu moral song, 239
The Christian and fortitude, 244

PART V

LIKE TAXES, DEATH

Christian death, 251
Baptized for death, 259
Alive to God, 264
Resurrection and
   triumphant tragedy, 268
Lift up your hearts, 274

PREFACE

BELLARMINE CHAPEL of Xavier University, in addition to functioning as a university chapel for the college community, serves also as the central place of worship for Bellarmine Parish, a small community of some one hundred families in the fairly immediate neighborhood of the campus. On Sundays, the Masses are attended not only by the resident students and the parishioners but also by a good number of transient churchgoers, who are attracted by the rather lovely chapel of moderate size and by the common conviction that Jesuits give good sermons. Since transient attendance over the years has been quite well maintained, it can be argued that the reputation for good sermons is justifiable—on the grounds that architecture alone would not continue to attract such crowds.

Now not all of the Jesuit fathers of Xavier University are regulars at Bellarmine Sunday Masses; most of the Masses are celebrated by about six of the priests, all members of the university faculty. Once in a while a particularly effective celebrant appears, who manages to acquire a much deserved reputation as a good homilist. In recent years, Rev. Thomas G. Savage, S.J., presently chairman of Xavier's Department of English, has acquired the reputation, among both students and parishioners, of being a good man to hear.

The following pages contain some of the homilies Father Savage delivered at Bellarmine Chapel from 1962 to 1971. Those of us who had the pleasure of hearing these as they were originally presented can scarcely fail to be delighted at their availability in permanent form for our occasional reading. Their treatment of matters of current interest, their clear and logical handling of the questions of the day, their terse yet forceful presentation of the arguments involved—all contribute to Father Savage's inimitable style.

For me, who have had the advantage of being a member of Xavier's faculty as well as a parishioner for some years, the publication of this volume represents an especially happy event. Admittedly, those of you who have not had the full experience of listening to Father Savage in the flesh must suffer an unavoidable loss—the stirring effect of his crisp, clear delivery at the chapel lectern and his almost childlike facial expressions preceding the adroit verbal statements that come crashing down on the mind. We more fortunate ones can almost supply the missing factor from our mind's eye and ear.

RICHARD J. GARASCIA
Department of Chemistry
Xavier University

APOLOGY

IF A PREACHER resembles an artist, his art depends upon two modes: oral technique and convincing associations between God's revelation and man's situation. In the sense that pulpit technique cannot be conveyed through the essay, the published homily seems a contradiction. The associations urged by a preacher, however, may perhaps be communicated through the written word.

A man preaches when he translates associations from his experience, both actual and vicarious, into homiletic expression. He moves from secular idiosyncracies to sacred significance. Neither a scholar nor a theologian, a preacher shares their attitude. But scholars and theologians speak to one another; preachers address congregants.

Unlike the painter or the novelist, a preacher's art is less terminal than seminal. A homily's conclusion depends upon the listeners' deeds. Questions raised by a preacher go unanswered not always because a preacher lacks wisdom, but simply because a preacher may not coerce. He speaks to men in a world of option; he does not serve as a chaplain at Walden II.

A homily discusses God's revealed word at a specific moment in history. The homily, then, relies partially upon contemporary mores and incident. A preacher strives to discern links between the human situation as recorded by the media and God's revelation in the Bible. A preacher must read and react; at times he must try to square the circle, that is, to contemplate amid activity. A preacher's reading and listening provide no surrogate for the actual, but augment his experiences in office, lounge, street, classroom, and conference table. Often vicarious encounters, however, with press and television, with cinema and poetry, so strike a preacher that they become part of his idiom. These homilies include actual and vicarious experiences of the preacher. Every effort has been made to cite the exact source of these experiences, but with the passing of time—eight years in some cases—echoes of literary encounters may appear undocumented. To those persons whose words evoked response, my gratitude for the inspiration, my apologies for a weakened and inadequate memory.

THOMAS G. SAVAGE, S.J.
Xavier University

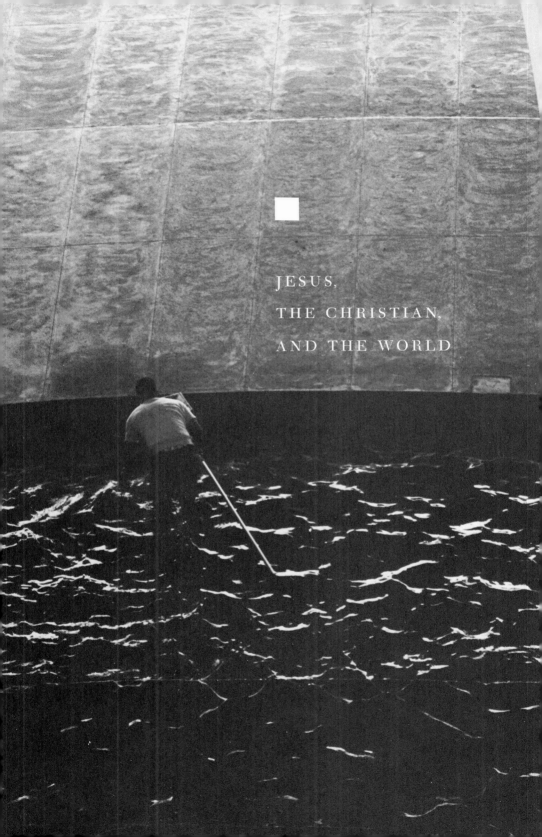

JESUS,
THE CHRISTIAN,
AND THE WORLD

I have fought the good fight to the end;
I have run the race to the finish; I have kept the faith;
all there is to come now is the crown
of righteousness reserved for me, which the Lord,
the righteous judge, will give to me on that Day;
and not only to me but to all those
who have longed for his Appearing [2 Timothy 4:7-8].

AND NOW A WORD

FROM OUR CREATOR

EVEN AS THE ARTIST, the preacher of the Word must ultimately rely on personal contemplation of the contemporary world as a source of inspiration. For if he is to relate God to the men of today, he must quietly read, watch, and listen to what is going on today. Karl Barth's suggestion that the preacher hold the Bible in one hand and the daily paper in the other would have to be extended today so that the preacher's grasp also included television, journals of opinion, and the popular press—underground and above ground.

The preacher's world, like God's world, demands more than theology, for it is a world of commerce and sport, of hippies and squares, of O'Connors and Goldbergs, of Notre Dames and Southern Methodists, of Harvards and Yales, of Funks and Wagnalls. A world of originality, a spare world, a world of counters and contrasts. And God, who speaks through human history, achieves the full significance of his Word through the word of men as revealed in this human situation. So man, for his part, must develop a critical sensitivity to the total world around him if he is serious about hearing a word from his Creator.

Our so-called Age of Aquarius, for all its supposed altruism and openness, actually reinforces a type of self-analysis and introspection that results, surprisingly enough, in a narrow personalism. It happens not so much because of any narcissistic bent on the part of Aquarians as from their unwillingness to reflect upon all aspects of a phenomenon or a situation before acceptance or rejection, an unwillingness to control that urge to respond to life according to emotional fancy or momentary whim. The Aquarian may well gather data, but he misses the reality.

In religious matters, for example, I have the impression that the Aquarian analyzes existence largely (if not exclusively) through his own eyes, seldom through the eyes of another, rarely through the eyes of God. And even when he does turn to Scripture, he refuses to listen to God's total word. He prefers

4

instead to select only those passages, those aphorisms and epigrams, those consoling parables, that confirm a casual response to religion and to life.

Yet it would be simplistic to say that religionists in the Age of Aquarius stress the word of man more than the word of God. The problem has deeper roots. It is not just a rejection of God's revelation; the problem rather is rooted in an impatience with anything that takes time, that requires contemplation. The word, be it God's or man's, requires reflection upon the data—and the Age of Aquarius may well be recorded as the age of superficial man, of the man who refused to listen. For despite the stress on dialogue today, a stress that would be encouraging in itself, fewer persons actually seem to listen anymore. And if a man is loath to listen to his fellowmen, it hardly surprises us that he cannot hear God.

Smothered by this visual and visceral Age of Aquarius, in fact, man grows suspicious of all words. He may even come to fear words. For words are difficult; words are ambiguous; words are delicate and fragile; words can upset. Dennis the Menace just recently exemplified this attitude perfectly. Margaret, his precocious playmate, used words that Dennis failed to comprehend, and so he cried in childish exasperation, "Who needs another word?" Since the problem centered on the use of synonyms, Margaret reminded Dennis that "lots of words mean the same thing." "Then why," said Dennis, "don't they get rid of them?" Let me add here that what especially frightens me about Dennis is the haunting fear that, should he ever matriculate, he will pursue the baccalaureate at Xavier.

Words should intrigue and stimulate our minds. Paul, for example, in his letter to Timothy, uses the image of an athlete to explain his situation. He says he has competed in a race, that he will receive the crown of a victor, that he has fought the good fight. It is an intriguing metaphor, one that makes a point both colorfully and concisely. But men are not supposed to take it literally, thereby identifying religious practice with participation in sport. Perhaps my own inadequacy piques me in this matter. After all, Billy Graham plays golf, even with presidents; Rex Humbard surfs in Hawaii; I don't know which end of the bat to hold. So the ridiculous identification of Christian asceticism and sport perplexes me. Muscular Christianity never works; history frowns upon the Crusades. Yet man continues to seek not mere parallels but positive identification of the athlete-saint, as interesting an oxymoron perhaps as that of scholar-athlete.

Some years ago, for instance, when Xavier University presented the Xavier Medal to Stan Musial— presumably because he exemplified a virtue of St. Francis Xavier—the choice was predicated on the flimsy assumption that St. Francis Xavier had been an athlete at the University of Paris. But track and field (the modern counterpart of Francis Xavier's assumed athletic activity) in the sixteenth century at Paris hardly resembled the Drake Relays. I find it

6

difficult to conjure up a vision of St. Francis Xavier jogging through the Bois de Boulogne and dodging the early-morning sweepers on the Champs-Élysées to stay in shape for a triangular meet with the Thundering Herd from Lyons and the Fighting Tigers of Alcala. Francis Xavier offers more to our world than a prototype for Stan the Man who made a quasi-virtue out of swinging from a crouch, that posture at the plate which our own beloved Pete Rose has sought, somewhat in vain, to emulate. The point is ultimately this: Paul's word is metaphor. To make it literal exploits the image and distorts the words.

Yet that penchant toward the literal, fundamentally, is the problem with Aquarians—for all their vaunted interest in navel-gazing and yoga meditation. What they see is what they get, and truth becomes a matter of personal whimsy or idiosyncratic imagination. They refuse to listen, or to look beyond mere appearances and superficial associations to a greater and richer reality.

This judging by mere appearances can be foolish, be it in life or in religion. Commerce thrives on unreflective man's ability to be maneuvered by unrelated associations and appearances. A manager of a gas station in Seoul, Korea, reported this week that his sales of gasoline are up thirty percent since he introduced girl pump attendants in hot pants. Patrons drove in, less for 260 Action than for reasons that had little to do with the petrol's superiority. Superficial associations, shall we say, accounted for these sales.

Judging by appearances can be embarrassing. In Rochester, New York, recently, a man pulled his car over to observe the scene of a traffic accident. A police officer told him to move along or he would be arrested. The man moved a few steps from the street to a private driveway and called to the officer: "You can't touch me now. I'm on private property." Big mistake. "I own that property," the officer answered and arrested the poor soul for criminal trespass.

Failing to penetrate appearances may be dangerous. In Blaydon, England, a man lifted floorboards in his home to investigate the source of a draft. He found a hole a thousand feet deep beneath the floor. It turned out to be an abandoned mine shaft over which he had lived unwittingly for twenty years. The wife said, "The room had always been drafty."

The point is that we all too often fail to investigate all sides of a situation; we settle for a partial view. Yet the man who follows an absolute rule like never betting on a front-running horse, or never playing a horse that lies off the pace, can make some awkward choices. A good handicapper considers track conditions, jockey, past performances on this track, distance of the race. Handicapping involves synthesizing the data; so does sensitivity to the human context of the word.

Take, for instance, the question of what precisely football contributes to a person as a person. We often hear about all the human values of football, especially on college campuses. In the latest issue of *Sport* magazine, Dick Kazmaier comments on his days as an All-American at Princeton, when he won the Heisman Trophy in 1951. "I talk about the benefits of football, how it teaches lessons not often taught today. Like discipline and team cooperation." The reporter concludes: "Those were lessons Dick Kazmaier learned well at Princeton." Lord, did he have to spend four years at Princeton to learn that? He could learn that by working in a foundry all week and playing in the Feldhaus League on Sunday. And to confuse the issue further, there is an article later in the same magazine quoting Tim Rossovich, a professional footballer: "It's pretty satisfying to hit somebody, feel him grunt, bounce him off the ground, see his eyes rolling around." I wonder if one also learns that at Princeton? A good street brawl might afford the same catharsis.

But are priests and religious any more immune to the pitfalls of failing to investigate all aspects of a situation? They, too, can proceed largely according to their own preconceptions in choosing apostolic approaches. In northern Michigan this summer, to take but one absurd example, a deacon working with young Indian children sought to teach them the use of the bow and arrow; he felt they should become practically aware of their heritage. The young braves, unimpressed, tore down the targets the deacon had erected. They wanted to play baseball. One of the older Indians was asked about this noble experiment of teaching the young Indians to shoot with bow and arrow as part of acquainting them with their cultural roots. "Well," he said, "that young fellow is making a mistake. You see, we tried the bow and arrow once and lost."

Ultimately man must strive to assess the totality of God's word in this world. God is dead, as Nietzsche said, because man killed him. St. Paul in writing to Timothy speaks of God as man's goal, as one who rewards and punishes, as one who assists human efforts. Too often in our efforts to blend the human and the divine, we create a religion without God, just as today's Aquarians seem to want a Jesus without the cross. Failing to respect the total word of God results in a church metamorphosed into a welfare agency, religious ritual turned into a sensitivity session or a rock festival. Worship becomes entertainment as the church strives to make things attractive and relevant, as if the sacrifice of the Mass had to compete each Sunday with the rerun of yesterday's Notre Dame game.

Remember that song of two years ago; "Look what they've done to my song, ma"? Sometimes I wonder, when I read about certain so-called religious attitudes toward life and morality and worship (and not all of them within the Catholic Church), if perhaps God, who has lovingly granted us the freedom to be ridiculous, isn't smiling to himself and saying, "Look what they've done to my word." Man may very easily distort the word of God into an empty humanism or a sterile sociology—especially if, in the Age of Aquarius, he refuses to penetrate appearances, ignores the fullness of the human situation and fails to listen to a word from his Creator.

10

The faithful all lived together and
owned everything in common; they sold their goods
and possessions and shared out the
proceeds among themselves according to what
each one needed [Acts 2:44-45].

JESUS DIDN'T KNOW POLYGLAS FROM POLIGRIP

THE CHRISTIAN attitude toward life may well be summarized in the single word *pilgrimage,* for in this life man is on route to another style of life that he can reach only through death. Consequently, the conclusion the Christian draws is: Life in this world is somehow or other incomplete. Thus, he figures life in terms of a journey, a trial, a probation, a preparation. Events of this life are judged by the Christian largely in the light of whether or not these

11

events help him or hinder him in the achievement of a completeness that occurs only at the end of life and after death.

Opposed to this basic approach is another fundamental attitude, that of the secular humanist who centers his attention exclusively on the events that occur in this world. The events of this world, in the mind of the secular humanist, as Rev. John Russell explains in his pamphlet "Is Humanism Enough?" are really the only actuality; they are the only reality for man either before death or after death. Man's destiny is largely the product of his own decisions made within his own natural environment and effected solely by the natural development in this life. Any desire on man's part for completeness after death, any craving on the part of man for something beyond this life, is made out of either ignorance or weakness. In the view of the humanist, such craving is hardly the lot of an enlightened man.

If my summary contrast of these two basic attitudes is correct, then Christianity and secular humanism are incompatible. Nevertheless, we find today a de facto attempt (whether or not it begins de jure is another question) to blend elements of secular humanism with Christianity. There are some, in other words, who take the value system of secular humanism and attempt to square this value system with the person of Jesus. Often enough, they begin rather with the value system than with the person of the Nazarene. They attempt to baptize secular humanism.

12

In this effort, man is frequently confronted less with an historical Jesus than with a Jesus of man's imagination. I don't say an imaginary Jesus, because certain elements of the historical Jesus are found when man brings his imagination to bear on creating Jesus all over again. What occurs is this: The elements from Jesus' own life are selected that are recognized as very practical for contemporary man. It is argued that since Jesus lived in this world, he was speaking to this world; therefore he must, some way or other, be relevant to this world.

So far so good. But the difficulty lies, I think, in the assumption that relevance always demands identification and, consequently, the more we can make this Jesus identify with our world (which is really putting the cart before the horse) the more relevant this Jesus will be.

It's true that Jesus knew the world. In his conversation with Nicodemus, Jesus says in effect, "Look, I've spoken to you about the material world and you haven't paid a bit of attention to me. How will you believe me when I talk about eternal things?" (John 3:12). Jesus knew the world around him, but Jesus hardly knew our world in the twentieth century.

Jesus not only was unaware of our world, he also did not identify himself with our world. Certain persons may act in a manner they identify with Jesus, but this differs from saying that Jesus is identified with these people. To declare, for instance, that Jesus really was the first hippie is to express an anachronism that is critically unsound, and one can no more identify Jesus with the Chicago Seven or the Catonsville Nine or the Milwaukee Five than one can with the valiant Six Hundred charging at Balaclava. One cannot identify Jesus that clearly with historical persons.

What these efforts attempt to do is take what Jesus may mean today before learning what Jesus actually meant in his own day and age. Yet if we truly wish to understand what Jesus means today, we must comprehend from the Scriptures what he meant at that historical moment when he lived. Otherwise, we tend to bring our imaginations to bear on *a Jesus* and to create our own Messiah.

There is a certain type of secular humanist, turned Christian, who would portray a contemporary Jesus as speaking over a Princess telephone, driving a Mustang, enjoying *Laugh In* or *All in the Family*. This effort, in one sense, is laudable. After all, man does want Jesus to speak to him today, here and now, in his language. But the precise difficulty is that Jesus did not live in the twentieth century. Jesus did not know that Coke is the real thing; he did not know that he has a lot to live because Pepsi has a lot to give; he could not distinguish Polyglas from Poligrip. He simply did not live in the twentieth century—and all these efforts to turn Jesus into someone who is very much at home with all the gadgetry of twentieth-century life are somewhat naïve and sophomoric.

Jesus has significance for us because he historically meant something, because historically he was somebody, not necessarily because we can use our imagination to make him relevant here and now. To know what Jesus means today we must know what Jesus meant. So the secular humanist, turned Christian, fundamentally errs in his effort to apply Jesus to his own historical epoch.

Jesus is simply not that closely linked with any one cultural attitude, with any one ethnic pattern. He is the Son of Man. He was born in a specific place, at a specific time, amid a specific culture and life-style, and this is part of the mystery of his person. But Jesus is not so idiosyncratic that he must always be linked with a specific day and age if he is to have significance. The life-style and culture of Jesus are less important than his person and his teaching; his beard less important than his words.

The error made by the secularist is that he tends to tie Jesus to *his* way of life, whereas man's response to Jesus must be such that it is compatible with Jesus' teaching and his person. Perhaps it is an oversimplification, but I would suggest that the secularist changes Jesus for his own day and age, whereas the Christian changes himself. Jesus has no need for metanoia, for change of heart, but man clearly does.

There was a time not too long ago when we all had the childish notion that someone along the line had the answers to most questions. A child often thought that this was the adult world: "If you don't know, ask your father," "If you don't know, ask your teacher," "If you don't know, ask the priest," "If you don't know, write your congressman." Somebody always had the answer.

In recent years, we have learned that we simply do not possess the full truth and are not likely to attain it in this life. We are realizing more and more that we are all gropers, we are all reaching. The difficulty is that some of us are not satisfied with groping; we want that here-and-now response. Some people turn from groping to griping, and since they find that Jesus and his Church are no longer giving the answers they like to hear, they eliminate Jesus and his Church from their lives. They eliminate worship; they eliminate the Christian ethic. Unwilling to grope in mystery, they would rather gripe against God and against the Son of God.

The secular humanist does not gripe against God. "Well now," he declares, "these once-cherished measures of value no longer are adequate to our life-situation." So what he attempts to do is make over Jesus into his own image. He identifies Jesus with a specific life-style.

Once a specific life-style is adopted for Jesus, however, man risks narrowing the person of Jesus. If we say that Jesus has only one life-style and we don't like it, we abandon him. The mistake, basically, lies in identifying Jesus solely with a specific life-style.

One can do this with a superficial view of Scripture. One can take a passage, for example, from the Acts of the Apostles about the early Christians holding all things in common, and one could defend

16

communism from that passage; but this is clearly not the same thing as saying that Jesus of Nazareth was the forerunner of Marx or Lenin or of the Soviet Union as we know it today. Still, this passage clashes with the capitalistic pattern of the United States of America in the twentieth century, so we might be tempted to say that Jesus and his message have no relevance for us today.

What can we do? We can go the route of the secular humanist and remake Jesus into our image. Or we can distill the essence of that teaching that transcends specific life-styles and introduce it into our way of living. We can live as a member of the institution that Jesus founded even if the accidentals of that institution are quite different from those of the early Christian community. The difficulty that faces man—especially the Christian—is whether he will turn Jesus into an image of himself or accept his person as it is.

Are we willing to go back in history, to read Scripture and try to understand what Jesus meant before we try to apply what he means today? That passage portraying the disciples on the way to Emmaus clearly exemplifies how some of them had an imprecise idea of Messiah, a notion different from what Jesus himself had taught. Jesus did not fit their image. Jesus may not conform to man, but man must try to conform to this person of Jesus if he is to be a Christian. In one of his epistles, Peter says that Jesus has been revealed in our time, in our day and age, but that he is from eternity (1 Peter 1:20). This is

17

the point we must always keep in mind: Jesus is transcendent. He is far more universal than any specific life-style.

It is interesting that Harvey Cox, after pretty much eliminating the contemplative life in his book *The Secular City*, has now restored a life of prayer to Christianity in his latest book *The Feast of Fools*. Which raises a few questions: Are we merely going from one fad to another? Are we merely leaping about, saying that now the emphasis is here and now the thrust is there? Or is there something transcendent, something universal, something in Christianity that does not depend on the feeling or the thought or the whim or the speculation of contemporary theologians?

Fundamentally the answer lies in Scripture; that is, man must return to Scripture to see what Jesus actually meant. Man must realize that there can be a variety of social and political systems, all of which may be sound Christian responses to the person of Jesus. Man must avoid, as the secular humanist has not, narrowing that life of Jesus to the extent that it can be applied in only one way at any one time in history. That is to miss the essence of the Nazarene.

I am the good shepherd; I know my own and
my own know me [John 10:14].

JESUS: GOOD SHEPHERD
OR GOOD GURU?

DIETRICH BONHOEFFER, who spoke of a secularized Christianity, lent a religious aura to secular humanism. He started a trend in 1945 that reached its
zenith in the United States with Harvey Cox's book,
The Secular City. Now this secularized Christianity
seems to have spent itself, for as the churches became more worldly, the people became more religious. One obvious sign of this religious interest is
the mystical revival that has occurred among the
young—an interest in the occult, in eastern religion,
even in such primitive practices as witchcraft.

Theodore Roszak in his recent book, *The Making of a Counter-Culture*, speaks of rock music and such pilgrimages as the Woodstock Festival as signs of this renewed interest in the transcendent. Pop songs like Simon and Garfunkel's "Bridge Over Troubled Water," with its gospel beat and soft tones, illustrate the desire for something beyond that material world to which the secular Christian wants to commit us and to limit us.

Rev. David Read, pastor of the Madison Avenue Presbyterian Church, has said that "the revolt against the secular and the materialistic society is in full swing amongst the young, and the traditional signs of yearning for the transcendent—apocalyptic imagery, ecstasy, symbolism, communes of withdrawal—are all around us."

This interest in the mystical and the occult often includes the guru or religious guide who leads one through transcendental meditation (what Jesus and those of us over thirty call prayer). Those inclined toward this approach, even when they may use drugs to induce certain states of soul, turn Jesus from a shepherd into a guru.

Perhaps there is reason for changing Jesus' image. If Jesus is shepherd, then Christians are sheep: that is, docile, easily frightened, helpless, incapable of handling themselves in tight situations, clearly in need of someone stronger, like a shepherd, if they are to survive. Such a portrait hardly inspires. Moreover, the notion of shepherd is too rural, too idyllic, too out of touch with the world to reach us.

20

On the other hand, the image of guru strikes us as contemporary and alive. A guru, too, like Jesus, reveals the secrets of life. Not through doctrine imposed from above, however, but through technique and process.

Man's response to a guru is largely, "What can I now do?" A guru prompts us to action now that we have been born again through his guidance. He has taken us off Dr. Pepper and put us on the needle; he has encouraged us to switch and not to fight, to substitute marijuana for Tareytons. The guru prompts us to get with it. In his hands we come alive.

This vitality appeals to man. Man likes to be active. A cartoon in the *Saturday Review* some time ago portrayed two medieval knights riding off to battle. One of them was saying: "Dragons or no dragons, anything's better than listening to shop-talk around that damn round table." A guru prompts man to act, and man revels in it.

A shepherd, on the other hand, hardly evokes such a response. One responding to a guru says, "What can I do?" One responding to a shepherd says, "What can I be?" The response to a shepherd is to join his flock, to be a member of the fold. It is less what a person does than what he fundamentally is: one must be before one does.

In one sense Jesus is both guru and shepherd, because both the response of man's being and the response of man's activity are part of Christianity. It is not a question, then, of either/or, but rather of which is more fundamental. Before one can become a do-er, he must become a be-er. Before one does something, he must first of all be somebody.

Christianity is more than a mode of life, more than a process of social engagement. A Christian is known not solely by what he does, but fundamentally by what he is. Membership in some way or other in the fold of the good shepherd is necessary; a sacramental life that transcends the material world is necessary. Scripture certainly supports Christian activism, but Jesus also said, "Unless you eat my flesh and drink my blood you have no life in you" (John 6:54). You don't even exist as a Christian without the Eucharist.

True, the parable of the Good Shepherd indicates that membership in a group is necessary for the Christian. For him, however, participation in activity with others must be motivated by love and supported by personal prayer, by sharing in liturgical worship, by being born anew in baptism, by being confirmed as a member of Jesus' fold.

The secular humanist places all his chips on social involvement, on activism. So the Christian who finds a total Christianity in activism stands at one with secular humanists. Love of neighbor, though it is admittedly an important part of Jesus' teaching, is not constitutive of the total Christian life. To declare that it is reduces Christianity to a single horizontal dimension, wherein only a relationship with the neighbor is possible. Man's vertical relationship to God can be effectively eliminated by the emphasis on activism in secular humanism.

Accordingly, we are ever in danger of omitting an important part of our lives as Christians if we go the route of the secular humanist. We resemble the Boy Scout who received a poor report card at school. He told his father, "I was so busy obeying the Scout code, helping old ladies, keeping myself physically strong, mentally awake, concerned for others, and morally straight, that I didn't have time to do my homework." We omit an important aspect of Christianity when we are so busy with activism that we never pray, never share in the sacramental life of Jesus.

If the Rev. Dr. Read is correct in his analysis, the tendency of young persons today is away from a secularized creed with its activistic emphasis and toward a sharing in prayer and in spiritual experience. Young persons are looking for that vertical dimension in their lives to serve as a source for the horizontal dimension.

There is truth in the contemporary cry "We are what we do." But first of all we are what we are. Before man does, he must first be. Before one *acts* as a follower of Jesus, he must *be* a follower of Jesus. Jesus, then, is not just a guru, for one accepts a guru's teaching but he does not find salvation in his person. One listens to a guru's teaching, but one joins a shepherd's flock. Jesus may well be a good guru, but more importantly he is a good shepherd.

A response to Jesus through membership in his flock is suggested by Peter in his words recorded by Luke in Acts 4:12. Peter emphasized not *what* was done, but *in whose name* it was done. Jesus, the cornerstone, was important.

We simply are not Christians without Jesus. And we cannot join Jesus without the sacraments and prayer, both of which the secular humanist and the Christian activist de-emphasize, if not positively eliminate. The image of the sheep and the good shepherd seems to express this better than the image of the guru. Thus it is the good shepherd who reveals to us our basic identity as members of his fold, as Christians, as persons first and foremost united with Jesus.

Render, therefore, to Caesar the things that
are Caesar's, and to God the
things that are God's [Matthew 22:21].

JESUS NEVER SANG

"THE STAR-SPANGLED BANNER"

ALTHOUGH not generally considered an aspect of
secular humanism, nationalistic attitudes which
practically equate the state's decisions with Jesus'
teaching tend to force Christianity into a chauvin-
ism that not only is opposed to Jesus' teaching but
also represents a type of secular thinking. In our efforts to prove that a good Catholic can be a good
American, we may unconsciously express an exag-
gerated notion of patriotism that leaves little room
for the Christian conscience to disapprove by action
what it does not morally accept. Church and state

are blended in Catholic schools very neatly. Primary schools exploit the glib phrase, "For God and Country." Youngsters recite the pledge of allegiance to the American flag after their morning prayer. ROTC units find a happy home on Christian campuses. And the Christian student who refuses military induction is considered by some to betray both his country and his God.

Nevertheless, such efforts at accommodating church to state may bind a Christian in a way that militates against his Christian principles. Jesus clearly distinguishes between God and Caesar. "Render, therefore, to Caesar the things that are Caesar's, and to God the things that are God's." Caesar is fundamentally finite, limited; the state is not God, and efforts to equate the state with God lead to a political situation not unlike that of the Soviet Union, where the trappings of revealed religion are exploited by the state.

Jesus certainly differentiated between the state, which is of this world, and his own kingdom, which is not. Moreover, Jesus did not live the American dream; he knew no pluralistic society; he was unaware of the delights of apple pie and of the flag and of fireworks on the Fourth of July. Jesus never sang "The Star-Spangled Banner."

Jesus did not spell out a political doctrine. Thus the rather ridiculous position of devout Christians who believe that God is always on our side, who never realize that such thinking leads to a secularism that is the direct antithesis of Jesus' teaching.

Lester Maddox, for example, leads a group of marchers carrying placards labeled "In God We Trust" at a recent march for victory during which hymns were sung that are associated more with the chapel than with the political arena.

True, politics, like all human activities, has its moral dimensions; but this does not mean that a state's decrees are God's laws. If there is no such thing as an unpolitical man, as Malamud urges in *The Fixer*, if the Christian is political, he is so only insofar as his moral code guides his political involvement. But the Christian who blindly complies with the state because he believes that Jesus is on his country's side can hardly be said to recognize Jesus' distinction between God and Caesar.

An intelligent Christian questions governmental procedures in the light of Christian principles. No president of the United States enjoys a charisma by right of his office; no politician by his election becomes a Christian spokesman. These men are finite, serving a finite institution, working with finite means for finite goals. So the phenomenon of Christians equating the law of the land with the teaching of Jesus hardly conforms to traditional Christian attitudes to the state.

Consider, for example, the Christian attitude toward war and peace, a most vital area today of conscientious dissent from official procedures. What has been the traditional Christian position in this matter? Has the state's word always been taken as the voice of God in matters of war and peace?

27

Jesus accepted the prophetic tradition that looked to an era of peace and love in which men would, in the words of Isaiah, "beat their swords into plowshares" (Isaiah 2:4). In the Sermon on the Mount, Jesus declared, "Blessed are the peacemakers, for they shall be called children of God" (Matthew 5:9). Jesus commanded us not even to be angry with others (Matthew 5:21-22). He said to Peter that "all those who take the sword will perish by the sword" (Matthew 26:52). Following Jesus' example, the persecuted Christian communities in the early Church responded to violence with nonviolent love.

From the first century to the fourth, most Christians would neither engage in Rome's military campaigns nor justify killing as a means to achieve one's goals. The non-Christian writer Celsus (A.D. 178) reproached the Christians: "If all men were to do the same as you, there would be nothing to prevent the king from being left in utter solitude and desertion." The writings of St. Justin Martyr, St. Clement of Alexandria, and St. Cyprian all bear testimony to the fact that the name Christian was synonymous with peace, that the martial Christian was a contradiction in terms.

A subtle change occurred in the year 313, when the Roman Emperor Constantine recognized Christianity as the official religion of the Empire. Now, for the first time, the Church became an institution closely linked with civil authority. And the barbarian invasions of the fourth and fifth centuries confronted Christians with this disturbing question:

"What would you do if someone tried to kill your family or attack your nation unjustly?" Now arose the doctrine of the just war. St. Augustine declared that since perfection was impossible in this world, consequently peace was also impossible in our life. Augustine said: "No one indeed is fit to inflict punishment save the one who has first overcome hate in his heart. The love of enemies admits of no dispensation, but love does not exclude wars of mercy waged by the good."

At the time of the Crusades, when many of those same barbarians had been baptized with a rather imperfect understanding of Jesus' teaching, the cross became not a sign of peace but a standard for battle. Pope Urban II spoke of the need for the Crusades with the battle cry: "Deus vult" (God wills it). [Few of us would quibble with the will of God; we cannot help but wonder, though, how the Holy Father in 1095 was so certain of his position in this very political matter.] The principles of the just war were shelved when inconvenient. The situation became so serious that in the thirteenth century Thomas Aquinas offered the following principles for just warfare: (1) It must be waged by a public authority for the common good; (2) a just cause is required; (3) it must be fought with right intentions; (4) the harm done by the war must not exceed the good that comes from it (the principle of proportionality). Even the most vigorous anti-Thomist will allow, perhaps, that these are workable guidelines and sound principles.

In the Renaissance, Thomas More called for a strict observance of these principles, and the Dutch moralist Erasmus condemned many of his fellow Christians for behaving "like hawks. . . . Christians tear each other like wolves. And who is responsible for all this? Not the common people, but kings . . . not the young but the greybeards . . . not the laity but the bishops."

From the sixteenth to the eighteenth century, three "peace churches" arose: the Anabaptists (now the Mennonites), the Brethren, and the Quakers. These groups have attempted, by their witness to peace, to render to God the things that are God's and to give what is due the state—and never to confuse the two.

Twentieth-century efforts to oppose war were likewise made by churches. In 1914 the Fellowship of Reconciliation was founded by Richard Roberts and Henry Hodgkin. In 1931, the Theological Convention of Fribourg restated the principles of a just war, and added that modern war was no longer a proportionate means among nations.

Nevertheless, Christians have tried to serve God by serving whatever cause the state embraces. In 1939, Roman Catholic clergy and hierarchy urged German soldiers to support their country and to do their duty in obedience to the Führer. The late Cardinal Spellman was not above a fervent exhortation to American troops at Christmastime.

The Second Vatican Council looked on war with a very modern attitude, an attitude interestingly enough that echoes the early nonviolent, nonpolitically oriented Christians who preceded Constantine. And in November 1968, the Catholic bishops of the United States questioned whether the action of our country in Vietnam had not already exceeded the principle of proportionality in warfare.

In the light of this cursory historical summary, it would appear that young Christians who are conscientious objectors can make out a strong case based on Christian principles. And yet a priest testified at a local draft board in Ohio not six months ago: "A Catholic cannot be a conscientious objector." How naïve. How secular. How insensitive to Jesus' distinction that gives Caesar only what belongs to him, but gives God what is God's. Such a denial of conscientious objection tends toward a secularism that is as crass as that of those who see no need for any sacramental system.

Our young men in Vietnam are not fighting for Jesus. They are battling for Caesar, for their country, for something finite. American wars ought not be turned into holy wars, into struggles between the enemy, the powers of darkness, and ourselves, the children of light. This attitude reveals at worst a militant secularism, at best a muscular Christianity, and neither of these was the approach of Jesus, who gave Caesar his due—but no more.

He entered Jericho and was going through the town
when a man whose name was Zacchaeus
made his appearance; he was one of the senior
tax collectors and a wealthy man [Luke 19:1-2].

THE IMPORTANCE OF

BEING ETHNIC

WHETHER any intrinsic link exists between the Age
of Aquarius and the increasing stress upon ethnic
roots seems a moot point. Clearly, however, Americans today tend to emphasize, rightly and wrongly,
their lineage and cultural heritage. Perhaps this ethnic stress rides the nostalgic tide engulfing us today.
Three current Broadway plays illustrate this strong
ethnic consciousness: *Unlikely Heroes*, a dramatiza-
tion of three stories by Philip Roth, concerns neu-
roses of twentieth-century American Jews; a musical

from Israel, *To Live Another Summer, To Pass Another Winter*, unfolds a capsule history of the Jewish people; stereotyped scenes from the ghetto form the substance of the play *Ain't Supposed To Die a Natural Death*. Theater reflects the strong ethnic patterns of our contemporary scene.

Respect for cultural heritage indicates a healthy reverence for history, literature, and art; but excessive emphasis on ethnic elements often leads to a stereotyping of races that is either unjust or uncharitable. Or even both. Zacchaeus, Scripture says, was a "tax collector and a wealthy man," a biblical hendiadys implying that people classified him, and other such officials, as extortioners. No wonder the people stood amazed when Jesus treated Zacchaeus with kindness. Our stereotypes blind us to a person's total value.

Ethnic stereotyping leads us to stupid assertions like the televised advertisement for Tetley's Tea: "The most popular tea bag in England." Certainly the British enjoy tea, but they scorn the tea bag as an American abomination. To say that a tea bag is the most popular in Britain is not unlike talking about the largest polar bear in the Amazon Basin or the greatest ice hockey player in Texas. Note that the ad, in its simplicity, appeals to an American's stereotyped view of the average Briton.

Significantly, one of the more popular televised comedies today focuses attention upon an ethnic bigot, Archie Bunker, whose comic pathos surges like a geyser from an ignorant heart that rests content with benighted and obtuse loyalties to unreal situations. Yet Archie resides somewhat within each of us when we ignorantly choose according to ethnic stereotypes. As one person remarked about the United Nations, "The trouble with the U.N. is that there are too many foreigners."

Certain hearty Saxon types in this country delight in that simplistic designation of the United States as "God's country." We are citizens of God's country neither more nor less than any German, Indian, Japanese, or Ghanaean is a citizen of God's country. The presumption here seems to be that God somehow signed the Declaration of Independence or passed it along to Moses with the decalogue.

The Catholic Church transcends all ethnic differences, while making allowances for the distinct cultural heritage each of us shares. Joining the Lutherans at Fountain Square to celebrate Reformation Sunday represents, in a tiny way, the recognition of our need to stress unity amid our differences. Such celebrations will hardly result in any dramatic acceptance of one church over another. And it will still be some time before a public school may be used for a Catholic liturgy as Princeton High School is being used today for a Lutheran service, but we nevertheless eagerly anticipate that moment when there will be neither Jew nor Greek, when unity will transcend mere ethnic factors, when the state will indeed be separate from every church.

What all this implies is that the cleavage in culturo-religious attitudes among us is as serious as the

34

stereotyping of persons or nations. The self-conscious ethnic implicitly longs for a simpler day in the past that will never occur again; the Jesus freak and other assorted Aquarians become so involved in the present moment they are blind to either past or future; the Catholic anticipates what Paul speaks of in his second letter to the Thessalonians, the *parousia*, that moment of personal and communal fulfillment at the end of time. The ethnic considers that this "City of God" existed only in the past; the Aquarian thinks that this city here and now is the only actual city; the Catholic understands that he begins a God-like life through sacramental grace here and now, though full sharing in God himself comes only after an individual's death.

It is as a consequence of this basic distinction in attitude that there arises the implicit belief that God somehow belongs only to a single nation, that the Church constitutes an insular corporation based solely on ethnic factors. This attitude clashes head-on with the word *catholic*, which describes the universality and transcendent element of the Church founded by Jesus. Religious roots are certainly associated with our ethnic roots, but the two are not identical. We stupidly impede the great work begun at Pentecost if we jettison the pluralism in Catholicism today.

An article by Professor Michael Novak in a recent issue of *Harper's* magazine opens with the author's cri de coeur: "Growing up in America has been an assault on my sense of worthiness. . . . I am born of

PIGS—those Poles, Italians, Greeks, and Slavs, non-English-speaking immigrants numbered so heavily among the workingmen of this nation. Not particularly liberal, nor radical . . . born outside what in America is considered the intellectual mainstream. And thus privy to neither power nor status nor intellectual voice." If this pitiable lament of the ethnic intellectual accurately portrays the cultural attitudes of many persons, then nothing can prevent such a person from walking absurdly into a cultural cul-de-sac.

Professor Novak's lament concentrates on feelings of estrangement among ethnics. "Of what," he asks, "shall the man of Buffalo think, on his way to work in the mills, departing from his relatively dreary home and street? What roots does he have? What language of the heart is available to him?" Mike Royko, the Chicago columnist, thinks that Novak's sensitivity reveals "an academic mind trying to comprehend" the concrete human plight. "I don't really think any one of us knows what the man in Buffalo thinks," wrote Mr. Royko, and he added that he probably thinks like the Alabama sharecropper, the Tulsa oil worker, and the ethnic in Warsaw and Moscow. On their way to work each morning, they are all probably more concerned with the weather than with themselves. In any event, as Mr. Royko observes, perhaps only a university professor starts the day with a thought like this: "Here I am rootless and out of the mainstream of American life, which is why I am notoriously taciturn, sullen, nearly speechless, and disinherited by the American dream." Novak really exploits the ethnic situation without offering the ethnic a wider vision, a truly catholic vision, which is what he needs.

The careful attention to one's cultural roots has a definite value, but if such stress only serves to focus upon ethnic differences or, what is worse, to develop ethnic stereotypes then such attention stands inimical to us as Catholics. The Church transcends all geographical boundaries, all purely ethnic differences. The people of God live everywhere in this world, not just in Price Hill or Finneytown or Grosse Pointe or Westchester County or in the rich farmland of Jasper, Indiana. It would be ironic if the Age of Aquarius, which presumably craves to unite us, should serve only to divide us further because of an awkward focusing on the purely ethnic distinctions among us.

We all need to eliminate our awkward attitudes toward any group or class, religious or ethnic. Such an acknowledgment hardly betrays our principles if our principles are genuinely catholic and universal to begin with. Ethnic roots provide variety and diversity, and only *this* is the importance of being ethnic. But variety and diversity hardly demand separatism or division—or what is most uncatholic, that unjust and uncharitable segregation of a person according to his ethnic roots.

I am not asking you to remove them from the world,
but to protect them from the evil one.
They do not belong to the world any more than
I belong to the world [John 17:15-16].

HOLDEN CAULFIELD AND JESUS:
CATCHERS IN THE RYE?

IN THEIR SONG, "7 O'clock News," Simon and Garfunkel softly chant "Silent Night" while a newscaster
recites the ugly details of the day's events—riots,
murders, war, and cheating. The song dramatically
contrasts the clash between the Jesus event and the
world event of ugly racism, uncharitableness, injustice, and a sterile nationalism that lies at 180 degrees
from the world of the carol hailing Jesus' birth.

There is no effective way to keep man from contact with the seven o'clock news, from knowing

man's inhumanity to his fellowman. Man inevitably learns evil no matter how innocent a child he is. Holden Caulfield, in Salinger's novel *Catcher in the Rye*, is asked by his sister Phoebe what his future plans are. Holden romantically avows that he wishes to be a catcher in the rye, one who keeps the children from running off the cliff. Holden simply wants to protect others from evil, as represented by his idealistic desire to remove crude graffiti from the nation's walls.

Perhaps every man wishes he could keep himself and others from harm's way, from being touched by the evil in the universe. Some men seek this protection in religion. They consider Jesus as a shield defending them from the onslaughts of sin. They want a Jesus who is largely a protector, a catcher in the rye, the forerunner of Holden Caulfield.

Such efforts at sealing off men from the universe are absurd, for there comes a time when each man realizes that this world neither is paradise nor was meant to be. Hamlet, upon first comprehending that something is rotten in the state of Denmark, remarks how weary, stale, flat, and unprofitable seem to him all the uses of this world. Hamlet has for the first time encountered another person's insensitivity. That his own mother reveals such cruelty only compounds the issue. Holden Caulfield likewise meets the world. And if his reaction is less poetic than Hamlet's, it says roughly the same thing: This world is filled with evil, with facades, with pretense; this world is phony.

Men erect these facades perhaps without even realizing it; it seems we were destined to act at times in a most contradictory way. Yet amid these facades, amid these pretensions, amid this phoniness, men must find God and serve their fellowmen.

Even the slightest incongruity reveals man's tendency toward the phony. A sign over an Iowa restaurant reads: "Chuckwagon Smorgasbord." I doubt that some Swedish immigrant was capitalizing on the spirit of the Old West latent in each of us; the owner simply didn't realize the awkward juxtaposition of the words. And we smile at the incongruity of a menu item: "South African Lobster Tails from the Waters of the Caribbean." Perhaps there are so many more serious matters in life that we do not advert to these slight verbal incongruities, and yet these inconsistencies are syndromes of the facades, the lies, the phoniness, the evil which our world presents.

Man looks for deliverance from this world. Hamlet contemplated suicide; more altruistically, Holden Caulfield wished to be a catcher in the rye. Jesus, too, was conscious of man's plight. Jesus, by no means blind to the world he had accepted, brought new life to those who have a tendency to turn from God. Yet Jesus was not simply a protector; he did not guarantee that evil would be kept from the door of his followers. Jesus neither suggested that we withdraw into a comfortable ghetto of pietism nor agreed to accept the world's system on its terms.

The secularized Christian looks on Jesus' message as that of a catcher in the rye. Jesus is the ethical leader protecting his followers. Jesus stood with the social outcasts. They were poor, somewhat unlettered, slightly dusty, perhaps even dirty. Yet here in the early life-style of Christians was belief, but no dogma; a gathering, but no institution; a structure, but no bureaucracy. The message and the life-style are attractive to the secularized Christian, who speaks as if twentieth-century man could literally return to such a culture. Even more disquieting in this somewhat narrow pinpointing of a Christian life-style is the implication that only Jesus' message is valid, not his person or his signs and miracles. The secularist substitutes the shadow for the substance, the life-style for the person.

An opposite response is the pietistic soul's consideration of Jesus' person as the great deliverer, the supernatural protector. The pietistic soul worries less about Jesus' message than about Jesus' power and miracles, and his inclination is to live passively, letting Jesus assume a role akin to Santa Claus or Superman. Whereas the secularist is man-oriented and somewhat sophomoric, the pietist is slothful and naïve. Neither position accepts the total Jesus: person, message, and signs.

Today we are part of a social and political system that, for better or worse, has power on its side. One reaction to this system is to bend with the wind, to follow the system in its every detail, even when this system has only the facade of respectability. When protesters in Chicago are denied a permit to demonstrate, there is no need to throw rocks at the police. Any native Chicagoan knows the permit has been denied so you can have an opportunity to bribe your local alderman. This is living with the system in Cook County.

Not all Christians wish to compromise themselves, and the younger the Christian, the less willing he is to submit. Still, neither do they wish to be blown about by every wind; they are willing to live within the system, even while not acceding to its methods. Rather than follow the Pied Pipers of either secularism or pietism, they learn to adapt their beliefs to the world around them. To live amid evil does not indicate approval of it.

So, while Christians may not wholeheartedly endorse the system rampant around them, neither do they cop out by trying to reproduce literally the life-style found in Acts 2:44-45. Nor do they simply cover their eyes with a fiducial act, like the pietist. Such Christians are ever aware of the need to participate and to share with others, to live a life of justice and charity. And yet they realize this is not as easy as the glib phrase makes it sound; they see their religion as part of the problem, not as a solution.

Fundamentally, we are face-to-face here with the mystery of evil. Man queries how the merciful God can permit even the facade of respectability to continue, the phoniness that exists among us. Why does not God become a catcher in the rye? There is no satisfactory answer to this question, any more than there is a satisfactory answer to the question why the Trinity permitted the Second Person to be nailed to a cross. Furthermore, man wonders why he appears powerless to change society for its own good. The humanist responds by saying that man *can* effect the change, by proper understanding of the world and by goodwill on the part of all; but such a view suggests that this world is a lasting city, it discards the notion that man is fallen and understands him to be merely unenlightened. The pietist sees religion as a solution through simplistic faith.

History, however, teaches that mere intelligence and goodwill do not necessarily solve man's problem with evil. With every new solution, more problems arise. Even the pill, that presumed symbol of emancipation, brings a few difficulties along with its answer to some maidens' prayers. For every scientific advancement, more complexities arise. The world of human relations grows more complex as it evolves, not simpler. And when the pietist opts for simple faith, he is thereby considering religion to be a solution—whereas religion is a part of the problem.

The secularist looks upon Jesus as a deliverer because Jesus' message contains maxims for human guidance. Yet Socrates, Cicero, Shakespeare, Lincoln, and Adlai Stevenson could also speak in an incisive manner. Why single out Jesus' message? The pietist seeks deliverance through devotion. Both are looking for Jesus to be a catcher in the rye.

But Jesus is no catcher in the rye; he is not an insulator from the real world. In his person and in his teaching, Jesus prompts man to see this world for what it will always be—an evolving situation moving toward greater fulfillment through the agency of man but under God and with God. In one sense we have more to learn from the humanist than from the pietist. Yet our limited world neither totally explains itself nor fulfills itself, as the secularist would have it. Its permanence is found in its relationship to its Creator.

All efforts at sealing men off from evil are benighted and unrealistic. God compliments man by endowing him with that freedom of the sons of God whereby man voluntarily chooses to live amid the difficulties of his situation in a way befitting one who shares with others the new life of Jesus. Not a catcher in the rye, not a shielder from reality, not an insulator from evil, Jesus reveals the need to face this world on its terms, to see the world for what it is, and yet to realize that this world is meant for us only insofar as it leads to something greater.

The pietist denies the real world; the secularist limits it. Both the pietist and the secularist blindfold men to the total situation. Jesus took a route different from either.

God blessed them, saying to them, 'Be fruitful,
multiply, fill the earth and conquer it.
Be masters of the fish of the sea, the birds of heaven
and all living animals on the earth' [Genesis 1:28].

JESUS AND ECOLOGY

MAN TODAY is increasingly made aware of his environment and of its effects on his life-style. Public
demonstrations of whatever stamp or purpose share
one common element: They all dramatize man's
concern for the quality of life. To center attention,
as some have done, on pollution alone is to narrow a
problem that has much broader implications. Since
Americans, though, account for thirty percent of
the world's pollution while constituting only two
percent of the world's population, it is understand-
able that some Americans focus upon antipollution

45

measures as the solution to the problem of environment today.

Secularized Christianity, in its turn, has acted as a catalyst in prompting a truly Christian concern with environment. The current term for this concern, *ecology*, first appeared in an English dictionary in 1873. Originally, ecology was only a branch of biology dealing with relations between organisms and their environment. As man progressed and realized that scientific advancement often introduced moral problems in human relationships, the word assumed a strong sociological dimension. Ecology now refers to man's total environment as influencing his life-style. Paul Shepard in the book *Subversive Science: Essays Toward an Ecology of Man* calls ecology a "way of seeing, a perspective on the human situation." Thus described, ecology is at least related to an ethic and a moral theology.

Ecology, therefore, refers to more than studies of ice as solidified pollution. Some naturalists and politicians, though, still tend to divert our attention from a complete ecology by identifying ecology with pollution. "When the polluted waters of the Northwest reach the Arctic," they ask, "what will be the effect on the poor polar bears?" Since the American public has never been known for its immunity to bathos or sentimentality, a good citizen might feel so inspired to preserve *all* life that he would be reluctant to swat flies at a picnic.

Since, however, ecology concerns our *total* environment, of which pollution is only one aspect, man's spiritual life ought to be considered in any ecological study or survey. It's time, in fact, for theologians to begin searching out the theological understanding of ecology. Our environment involves more than clean air and pure water. Environment influences life-style, and an environment that encourages an immoral life-style pollutes man more than the spraying of DDT on plants. Immoral practices in housing, neighborhood adjustment, education, business methods, all affect our life-style. And all these areas, quite obviously, have a very definite spiritual dimension.

A clergyman who involves himself in this question is, as in other areas, damned if he does not speak and damned if he does. If the clergyman emphasizes the goodness of God's universe and man's need to seek first the kingdom of God, he is accused of devoutly burying his head in the sand. Should he invoke God's command to master the universe, he risks the accusation of selling out to the technologists who certainly have followed that injunction of the Deity.

Nevertheless, a Christian must assume a position on ecology. But any Christian discussion of ecology must emphasize the total environment of man—home, neighborhood, campus, office, boardroom. Actions in these areas influence man more than the air he breathes or the water he drinks. Ecology's spiritual dimension needs recognition.

Ecology is incomplete if applied solely to the material matters of man's environment, to the technological aspects, to problems of pollution. It means more than removing litter; it demands more than controlling smog. To consider ecology solely in terms of disease control puts man in the same category as a fish who swallows an insect. The fish is doing its bit to control pollution, surely, but it hardly has a broad ecological concern. Man must move beyond mere pollution control and population control to a concern for his total moral and spiritual environment.

Fundamentally, man must respect the universe and the good things present in it. "And God saw that it was good." Man's use of the good things must not be callous or cruel, but considerate. But along with this attitude must go an appreciation for the things of the spirit. The undergraduate who takes greater delight in racing his three hundred horses down I-75 than in reading a challenging book certainly adds to the pollution about us. But what is worse is his hierarchy of values.

In discussing the spiritual dimension of environment, the Christian should not look to Jesus for a specific blueprint, for some program. Jesus was no bureaucrat in the habit of composing white papers on every subject. Jesus is hardly the forerunner of Ralph Nader. What Jesus does reveal is a respect for the universe and for man's mind. He shows an appreciation and a concern for spiritual things. Here, at least, in a concern for the total environment, Jesus and the genuine ecologist agree.

But, as a man dedicated to God, you must
avoid all that. You must aim to be saintly and
religious, filled with faith and love,
patient and gentle [1 Timothy 6:11].

NOT THE RAP,

BUT THE MAP

AN ITEM IN THE NEWS recently read: "Career ap-
parel, glamor uniforms for white-collar workers, is
likely to become one of the biggest markets for gar-
mentmakers in the next five years." The garment industry estimates that sales may total roughly $700
million annually. What this brief item reveals is yet
another instance of commerce's superimposing an
external code of conformity upon man, largely for
the sake of materialistic gain. Commerce wants not
only man's soul, but also his external appearance.
More significantly, this news item suggests that man

tends more and more toward emphasizing extrinsic process and procedure, specifically as found in his dress. Man stresses procedure over content and substance; that is, man today inclines to emphasize the rap, not the map.

In at least two cultural developments does this emphasis upon process (or upon the current syndrome of process, the rap session) appear. First, the attitude that history largely unfolds a process extrinsic to man. Secondly, what may be called an inversion of reason.

Ignorance of historical data and a disdain for historical interpretation of the contemporary scene are symptomatic of this so-called Age of Aquarius, a point made quite forcefully by William V. Shannon in a recent New York *Times* editorial. Our cultural malaise, one of whose effects is a denigration of history's role, has developed, Mr. Shannon observes, from intellectual trends that began with the arrival of the Industrial Age among western nations.

History can well be construed as the accumulated burden of man's past actions, a notion that may prompt a man to echo Yeats' theatrical declaration: "I spit in the face of time that has transfigured me." Time looms as the enemy. Even a cursory view of history reveals that during the late Middle Ages, when faith in life after death began to wane, time as a concept unrelated to eternity preoccupied man. Time as an absolute to be conquered paralleled a Renaissance notion that man solves his mystery without God.

The idea of time has ever concerned artists, from the elegiac poets of the Anglo-Saxon period with their stress on life's transiency that makes sense only in the light of immortality after death, to Robert Frost's dreamy question: "What to make of a diminished thing?" that is, what to make of a life that begins to die the moment it begins to live. Since, however, the economy—that ever-present dictator of things human—was largely agrarian at that early age, man had no choice but to order his life according to the seasons of the year.

With the Industrial Revolution, continues Mr. Shannon, life geared itself to the artificial pace of technology. Technology superimposed a new process on man's life. At first such procedure appeared harmless, as process always does to those unwilling to recognize its philosophical and theological implications. If man worked in a factory, man simply adjusted himself to the machine's rate.

Gradually, however, technology's pace invaded every cultural corner. The values of the factory—that is, efficiency, speed, total use of available resources—ultimately influenced man's domestic life. Man grew impatient, unwilling to wait either for a hamburger or the second coming of Jesus. The delayed reward of Christianity struck man as ridiculous. Instant culture, instant salvation, the gospel of the utopian humanists spurred by technology's advances, loomed as a distinct possibility. Man simplistically believed that through technological process he conquered time.

Consequences of this attitude appear today in many ways, as Shannon points out. Minimal speeds are enforced on expressways for example. Within the home, food-processing has made it possible for instant dinners to give the lie to the idea that a meal, no matter how ambitious, requires effort, time, or painstaking preparation. Technology now produces bread, for instance, that guarantees a child's growth during his wonder years, though it tastes like a blend of cotton and sandpaper. Processed chickens and turkeys have the flavor and texture of cellulose. Hamburgers taste like plastic discs. Everything may be processed, premixed, freeze-dried, franchised, and, most importantly, instant. "It don't taste good, but it sure saves time." And it was time man wanted to conquer, for time had by now become his absolute—since he had eliminated eternity.

Finally, observes Mr. Shannon, other cultural developments stem from the speed and efficiency of technology. Television, which has replaced books and radio, has made man instantly aware. Television may be adversely criticized for the violence it portrays, but its more subtle debilitating influence appears in its ability to render man aesthetically inert and to condition him to expect instant satisfaction. Within thirty minutes man has the news, editorial comment, and even entertainment as he takes five—or is it ten?—with Rosemary. Then it is over. No waiting; no time lost. Processed culture is efficient indeed.

More significantly, television conditions man to believe that life is merely procedure. Politics, to take one area, becomes a happening, a demonstration, a dramatic confrontation—all specific types of procedures, in themselves implying neither substance nor content. The entire business is largely rap, little or no map. Such technological procedures imply that our complex human society can be manipulated merely through process, not through painstaking thought and effort.

A corollary to this historical naïveté, rooted in the centuries-old humanistic rejection of man's eternal goal, concerns man's resentment of death—one process man has as yet not conquered. In controlling time through technological efficiency, man has numbered himself as victim. In rejecting the data of the past, as Aquarians do de facto if not de jure, man deprives today of any meaning tomorrow. Relationships are torn asunder because everything is mere temporal flow. No wonder Aquarians lack unity or synthesis. Life for them is constituted solely by a procedural time divorced from history. To conquer death, Jesus had to enter time. God had to become part of human history to bring man promise of fulfillment. To share that promise, a Christian must see himself not as a discrete particle of time, but as part of human history developing toward the eternal.

The second cultural development is the inversion of reason or the inversion of nature. The poet Alexander Pope, in discussing the artistic vulgarity and the lack of discriminatory taste in Timon's villa, crystallized this notion of inverted reason, inverted nature, in his couplet:

The suffering eye inverted nature sees;
Trees cut to statues, statues thick as trees.

When man grows vulgar, he subverts proper order, which depends on content as well as on method. In lieu of content or principles of philosophy, man concentrates on process.

A faculty member remarked to me once, "Do you really feel that you can go to the top on this campus?" My response was simply, "Why go to the top?" Will going to the top for some sort of procedural change make me a better teacher, enable me to be more available to students? The top usually is so busy talking to itself that no one there would really comprehend the problem I might have. "The fault, dear Brutus, is not in our stars, but in ourselves that we are underlings." More germane to my point, there lies behind this person's query the notion that the success of any effort belongs largely with those who control the process, not with those who control the content. In athletics, when a team fails to win, the usual solution is to fire the manager or the coach.

This inversion of reason appeared implicitly in a two-page advertisement in *Look* magazine some time ago, an advertisement concerned with drug education for teen-agers. The entire ad presumed that knowledge necessarily leads to execution, a naïve notion that Ovid blew sky-high when he de-

54

clared for all of us: "I see the better thing, I approve of it, and I choose the worse."

In this advertisement, the questions asked of parents were exactly the same as those put to teenagers. What was most interesting was the summarizing paragraph on each page. Note the implication in both situations. To parents, the ad (which was paid for by a federal bureau) suggested: "If your child's answers disturb you, it's high time you sat down together and had a talk about drugs." In other words, parents ought to have a rap session with their children, out of which the truth will be clearly apprehended and sound moral choice will follow. The dialogue itself will prove salvific. To teen-agers the ad argued: "When it comes to the drug scene, a lot of parents really don't know what's happening— as you may be able to see by their answers to these questions." More's the pity. In other words: "You kids are really a lot smarter than your dumb parents, but since you can't communicate with them because of their benighted obtuseness, send to your everlovin' Federal Government and we'll give you this booklet that will straighten out your poor parents who haven't a clue about where it's really at."

The implication seems clear: children control the parents, the prisoners control the guards, the inmates run the asylum. In brief, reason has been inverted. Rational order has been so distorted that what twenty years ago was comical is now the accepted pattern: "Son," the father said, "you're getting to an age when we have to have a heart-to-heart talk about the facts of life." "Sure, Dad, what do you want to know?" It's the Age of Aquarius, when process has replaced content, when dialogue has replaced philosophical principles, when man has replaced God, when reason has been subverted.

The rock opera *Aqualung* illustrates this inversion. On the jacket of the record, the assumption behind *Aqualung* has been written in Gothic script. It is an inversion of the Book of Genesis: "In the beginning man created God; and in the image of man created he him." And an echo of this inversion is repeated in the refrain of a song from *Aqualung*, "Locomotive Breath." The refrain has it: "Old Charlie stole the handle and the train won't stop going—no way to slow down." The refrain emphasizes again the largely horizontal process of human affairs divorced from content. Or perhaps the process is the content. The medium is the message. Movement, pace, process—but no substance. And why? "Old Charlie stole the handle."

A few years ago we heard in another pop song that "the pump don't work 'cause a vandal stole the handle." When the vandals stop the pump, the source of the power, nature is inverted. Nature is inverted when process supersedes content, when the rap becomes the map. Paul's letter to Timothy— with its emphasis on substantial matters like faith, integrity, and good works—suggests that in addition to the rap, man better also have a map. Man better know where he's headed. Only the map, and not the rap, provides the needed guidance.

56

That is why I am reminding you now
to fan into a flame the gift that God gave you when
I laid my hands on you [2 Timothy 1:6].

NOT THE MAN,
BUT THE PLAN

A COROLLARY to the spirit of "inverted nature" appears in certain contemporary cultural turnabouts. Bishop Sheen recently called attention to some concrete examples of this inversion: After nuns abandoned long habits, girls dressed in maxicoats; when some Catholics laid aside their rosaries, other people began to wear beads around their necks; religious prayer became passé, only to have people seek ecstasy through drugs; seminaries and schools abandoned traditional discipline, only to have street mobs adopt it to control their members through coercion; the Church adopts a sociological orientation, while salvation is preached by the "Jesus people."

This last turnabout illustrates an interesting phenomenon in the Age of Aquarius: the tendency among some to follow the man, but not the plan. The man is Jesus. The plan is his Church, with its authority, teaching, and sacramental system, the valid means for achieving full Christian fulfillment and eventual happiness and salvation.

Jean-François Revel's best seller, *Without Marx or Jesus*, develops the idea that revolution in the United States has come about not by our following any doctrine from the past, but largely through each person developing independently. In Revel's interpretation, neither the Marxian dialectic nor the Scriptures really influenced the revolutionary direction of the American people today. He points to the religious element present in American culture, which he calls a satisfaction of the "need for sacredness," and argues that today such satisfaction is sought largely in hit-or-miss adaptations of Oriental mysticism, or in a return to the Indian cult of natural foods, or in a superficial attachment to astrology. Above all, religion in America, Revel declares, has its roots in that old Yankee principle: the best religions are those you find for yourself. Today this phenomenon readily appears in persons who attach themselves to the man, Jesus, without reference either to his total person or to his plan.

The Jesus people in the Age of Aquarius have largely eliminated any genuinely historical ap-

58

proach to Jesus. They have latched onto him as they would to any contemporary hero. What they say about Jesus differs little from their reactions to Elliott Gould or Dustin Hoffman or Peter Fonda. Jesus fascinates them, but they observe the shadow of the man and casually overlook the substance of his credentials and of his historical work.

Paul writes to Timothy about the laying on of hands and about the grace of the Spirit, two important elements in Christian living that seem, at least implicitly, eliminated by the Jesus freaks. Scriptural imposition of hands demands an institution, something extrinsic to the purely personal response. The Jesus people, however, place their emphasis rather upon personal response. And Paul's "grace of the Spirit" implies that God gives an impetus to us, that our efforts are a joint process between God and man, not solely the individual's effort. As we know from other scriptural sources, God's grace ordinarily comes to us through that system we call the sacraments, those external symbols of God's work within man and among men. But when one eliminates systematic religion or the official church institution, one must overthrow as well those means Jesus established for the grace of the Spirit to reach man.

Jesus' plan included the cross. Therein lies the crucial test for the person whose religion is merely a vague response only to the man Jesus. They pick up Jesus, but not his cross; they follow the man, but not the plan. Christians who want no tough doctrines from a teaching Church, Christians who opt for a moral permissiveness that encourages a libertinism contrary to the decalogue, Christians who want communion with God without offering sacrifice to God—all these want the man without the plan, they want Jesus without the cross.

Admittedly, there are some masochistic souls who want the cross without Jesus. Those who demand law and order without humane reasoning, those dedicated to the state at the expense of the individual, those who talk about discipline for its own sake, about self-denial without a higher, more significant goal—all these want the cross without Jesus. But the cross without Jesus leads to pogroms and gas chambers; Jesus without the cross leads to effeminacy and sentimentality. Both are necessary: the man and the plan; Jesus and the cross.

Paul writes Timothy about accepting a structure, a plan, along with his response to the man. The two work together. The incomplete vision of Jesus eliminates his plan while wholeheartedly endorsing his person. It is an easy course to call oneself a Jesus freak. Such admission demands little doctrine, no historical comprehension, but only a loose commitment wherein nothing substantial appears to which one commits oneself. The Jesus freak may well exemplify what Jean-François Revel calls the "need for sacredness" within man. But the way he satisfies this need hardly squares with the Bible, which urges not only response to the God-Man but also acceptance of his divine plan.

THE CHRISTIAN:
HIS FAITH
AND HIS CHURCH

Since self-indulgence is the opposite of the Spirit,
the Spirit is totally against such a thing, and it is
precisely because the two are so opposed that you do not
always carry out your good intentions [Galatians 5:17].

LED BY THE SPIRIT

OFTEN IN HIS LETTERS, St. Paul speaks of the opposition between being led by the flesh and being
led by the spirit. He quite definitely declares that the
genuine Christian is led rather by the spirit of God
than by the flesh of man. Historically, we know, the
opposition between the spirit of God and the flesh
has provoked varying human responses. The medi-
evals considered "the flesh" the great enemy to the
following of the spirit; perhaps in some cases they
thought the flesh actually evil in itself. The Renaissance developed the idea that the flesh, like any

creature, was neither necessarily evil or even an evil influence, but good. Nevertheless, man needed to exercise self-control in observing the hierarchy of spirit over flesh.

For the past twenty years there has developed a renewed cult of the flesh in western civilization. The more subtle spokesman for this attitude is a type of existential philosopher; its more crass advocates are the pseudosophisticates who subscribe to the *Playboy* philosophy. These voices inform us that the flesh is not only good but is to be adorned, cared for, catered to, perhaps even worshiped. Assuming that any and every human activity is good, especially as a response to a personal need, these men teach that no genuinely human action is morally reprehensible.

St. Paul, however, distinguishes very clearly the gifts of the spirit and the effects of the flesh. Paul gives us both a litany of virtues, the fruits of the spirit of God, and a litany of vices, the effects of heeding the voice of the flesh. For example, love is a gift of the spirit, fornication is a gift of the flesh.

Problems arise today, though, when new apostles argue that fornication is in reality love. Also, drunkenness and debauchery, fleshly effects according to St. Paul, are declared to be human experiences called LSD trips and pot parties. Thus, what was an effect of following the flesh has been neatly turned into a gift of the spirit.

Now the hippie ideal of bringing love more and more into our world may be laudable, but their means are suspect precisely because they have indiscriminately identified all gifts of both spirit and flesh. And this hippie attitude is found not only in the Haight-Ashbury district of San Francisco; it is found in Kokomo and Kalamazoo. There is no need to live in Greenwich Village to discern this hippie philosophy; it prevails in the thinking of youths at local high schools and in the colleges and universities. Even if the external dress of local students may not resemble that of their Pacific Coast counterparts, their basic attitudes are the same.

Thus, in religious matters we may have reached a point where the gifts of the flesh are not always distinguished by sincere people from the gifts of the spirit of God. It is a situation that results necessarily, I think, from the greater emphasis currently being placed upon individual responsibility in religious observance. This is not entirely a bad thing; in fact, I personally think it is a good thing. But since more and more emphasis in one's spiritual life is being placed rather on individual responsibility than on ecclesiastical fiat—for example, abstaining from meat on Friday—there is a greater need for the individual to be able to distinguish for himself the gifts of the flesh from those of the spirit of God, unless that individual has already determined that today there really is no difference.

To discern the spirit of God in human activity, there are several options open to an individual. He might, first of all, rely totally on himself—his own reasoning, his basic interests, his own emotional reactions to situations. Explicit documentation is scarcely required here to support the observation that many people today conduct their spiritual lives in such a fashion. Fundamentally, they are optimistic romantics like Rousseau, like Huck Finn, like Holden Caulfield. Since in their opinion all institutions corrupt man, they have determined to follow only their own instincts in any moral matter.

Secondly, a person may follow another guide, some third party. He may accept the Federal Government or the city council as his spiritual guide, informing him that the proper moral attitude is contained in the civil law of the land. Or his guide might be a publication which is, for this individual, like to the Gospel itself. So his moral decisions are based on what he reads in *The National Review* or in *Commonweal* or in the *National Catholic Reporter* or the *Saturday Review* or *Playboy* or the *Christian Science Monitor*. Finally, this sort of individual may rely totally on what a priest or a minister or a speculative theologian tells him. Some individuals enjoy following a kind of moral Pied Piper as if he were the Messiah himself, especially if his inspired pronouncements happen to agree with the individual's own personal feelings and reflections. For some, a man of the cloth who presents novelties that totally disregard any and every tradition is considered a man of brilliant new insights. For others, a priest who insists on a slavish following of practices no longer binding is considered to be preserving the genuine heritage of the true faith. It really depends, usually, on the attitude of his followers and what they want to hear.

The third option is probably the least popular guide to discernment of the spirit today—namely, the teaching Church of Jesus Christ. The teaching Church is neither our own personal reflections nor the latest speculations of brilliant men, but the clear and explicit teaching of that Church founded by Jesus of Nazareth to be his moral and fiducial witness throughout history. Acceptance of this Church as a guide to the spirit may not always be personally as satisfying as following our own thought patterns or emotional reactions. Following the spirit through the teaching Church lacks the romantic derring-do one can exhibit in following an avant-garde theologian, or in reading a facile publication that purports to be reporting all sides of a question when it shows itself only in opposition to the status quo.

Being led by the spirit of God through the teaching Church requires an entrance into mystery, and contemporary man fears mystery. Ignorance always breeds fear, and in the mysteries associated with God man is ignorant of explanations satisfying to the rationalistic bent of twentieth-century intellects.

In his attempts to follow the spirit of God, contemporary man differs from ancient man in this at least: he does not like a God wrapped in mystery. He doesn't like the spirit; he likes the flesh. Ancient peoples, a-intellectual as they may have been, believed that the more they knew about God, the less mystery there was—and they believed mystery to be a very part of the Deity. Thanks to the scientific enlightenment of later generations in the western world, we have decided that as intelligent people we are entitled to know all secrets of the spirit. Consequently, when we encounter mystery, we reject it as irrelevant, silly, ridiculous, meaningless.

Scientific achievement has so overwhelmed us that, if we cannot put the puzzle together, we decide either that too many pieces are missing or that there really is no puzzle at all. Science, which has effected rapid change and swift intellectual advancement in our world, has made us most impatient of mystery, for mystery demands contemplation, and we feel the urge to keep moving. There is a certain validity to Robert Frost's description of science as "a 100-yard dash followed by a pole vault." In our scientific world, who has time for mysteries of the spirit?

It is our personal task to select a guide enabling us to discern the movements of the spirit. Should we select our own insights as the guide, we must have the honesty to say that we are ready and willing to defend them to God himself. Defending them to the country-club set really does not count. We must be prepared to defend them before God.

Should we decide to be guided in our morality by a third party, like the government or a printed publication or a theologian, we ought to be willing to present cogent reasons for accepting their word rather than our own. Reasons that will convince ourselves, other men—but above all God himself.

Finally, if we choose the teaching Church as our guide, we also run the risk of not thinking for ourselves, of letting authority dictate to us. The teaching Church is not capricious; she has her reasons for her teaching—but we may fail to think the reasons through. The advantage, I would suggest, is that defending the teachings of Christ's visible witness to God himself may be easier than defending either our own visceral rumblings or the speculations and decisions of a human third party.

Following the spirit of God in the concrete is difficult. It demands that we do two things which clash head on with the activist philosophy prevalent today. If we have joined the Pepsi generation in the hopes of really coming alive, we have quite possibly already given up these two necessary things: reflective reading and prayer. For discernment of the spirit of God demands careful study, the ability to distinguish the genuine from the sham, to separate reality from mere appearance. If we fail to take time for prayer and reflection, and so act solely upon our own instincts, we will resemble that very self-satisfied gentleman who began to comment vigorously on the extremely poor job of taxidermy that had been done on the parrot in the local barbershop. At which the parrot cried, "Says who?"

Only the prayerful, thinking Christian will distinguish the appearance from the reality. Only such a Christian will fully realize the difference between the gifts of the spirit of God and those of the flesh.

How rich are the depths of God—how deep his wisdom and knowledge—and how impossible to penetrate his motives or understand his methods! [Romans 11:33].

THE UNDERGRADUATE
AND MYSTERY

A MYSTERY is a fact that our reason alone is power-less to apprehend. Even revelation does not so ex-plain the story that our minds immediately grasp its full significance clearly. Confronted with the mystery of the Trinity, the triune God, a theologian may work to show that no contradiction between the one nature and the three Persons exists; he can-not reason to the Trinity's existence. St. Paul in his letter to the Romans says succinctly: "How rich are the depths of God!"

70

Those depths of God, though, are intriguing to the human intellect. And the university community, to which rational inquiry is fundamental and essential, must attempt to the best of its ability to penetrate mystery. What is important is that the university community maintain a proper approach to mystery.

One problem facing the university community is that it may well be oriented in the direction of knowledge and understanding, both of which are vital and necessary, but it fails to direct itself toward complete wisdom, natural and supernatural. Knowledge offers information; understanding enables man to see relationships; wisdom gives a man true insight.

Too often, however, wisdom is identified with insights that hardly differ from the attitude of the con man. Such wisdom is incomplete wisdom, because it offers insights only into the ways of the world. It is not unlike natural cunning. And the problem with relying on natural cunning or worldly wisdom alone is that such cunning can usually be met head on by the natural cunning of another. Then the search for wisdom is reduced to a battle of wits between two minds striving for wisdom without the aid of any outside source or direction.

It is like the counterfeiters who printed a number of bills of an $18 denomination. Suddenly they realized it would be difficult to pass these $18 bills. One of them said, "I know where we can unload these bills. Let's go to the hills of West Virginia. The people down there won't know the difference." Off they went to the hills of West Virginia and stopped in a town, not much more than a widening in the road, where there was a country store. The two worldly-wise counterfeiters entered the store and said to the old proprietor, "Say, fella, could you break some $18 bills for us?" "Sure thing," he replied. "You want it in three sixes or two nines?"

In general, there are two extremes to avoid in discussing a mystery like the Trinity. One extreme is the declaration that all study leads ultimately nowhere; so merely believe, say your prayers, and forget it. This pietistic approach, alien to a university community, is clearly a-intellectual. The other extreme is represented by the self-wise inquirer who believes himself equipped to rely solely on his own personal intellectual assessments of mystery. His danger is that he will grow smugly indifferent, proud, self-satisfied, and probably quite agnostic about mystery. He fails to see the validity of revelation, and he relies solely on himself.

Now a university runs the risk of valuing ideas arrived at by men alone. Undergraduates treasure them. No critic, no professor, no book, no institution, no church has told the undergraduates these things, so they can easily grow enamored of the fruit of their own search. In science, in history, in literature that may be foolish without proving fatal. But in matters of God, in theology, man needs revelation. The depths of God are too rich for man's natural powers.

The self-wise inquirer, though, dispenses with all outside sources of knowledge. He is impatient with mystery; he is intolerant of revelation; he rebels against a teaching Church in matters theological. Alone he wishes to search for truth; alone will he find complete wisdom. Yet his attitude is hardly a new phenomenon. Many people at the time of Jesus required a further sign according to their preconceived notions of the Messiah; many Greeks sought something more subtle than the earthy God-Man and the mystery of a God nailed by men to a cross.

A man generally assumes this attitude of the self-wise inquirer in high school, or at least by college. It is a period in his life when he begins to ask searching questions for the first time. And it may happen, if he is not directed and guided, that this young man will believe he is the first person ever to encounter the insoluble problem of man's freedom and God's omniscience.

The self-wise inquirer, unless he is intelligent enough to accept revelation, soon begins to murmur against any teaching with which he does not agree or any teaching that is uncomfortable for him because he cannot accommodate it to his way of life. Rebellion arises against the Christian conscience, and a proud arguing against the truths of revelation results. Doubt, scoffing, cynicism, skepticism, even apostasy may result.

If the self-wise inquirer persists in this attitude, he may become his own worst enemy. Far from growing in complete wisdom, he degenerates into a self-centered individual satisfied only with his own arguments and his own conclusions. It is the occupational hazard of the university community that members may make their own intellects the sole measure of all truth, even theological. Our wisdom may become largely egocentric.

Such a self-wise inquirer can even become an academic con man if he fails to realize that, when he approaches Christian mystery, there are elements which are not intended for total satisfaction of the agnostic intellect. The mystery of the Trinity, for instance, overwhelms us. We fail to comprehend. And what such a mystery suggests is that we not put all our chips on worldly wisdom alone and become slick artificers in matters of this world. The Trinity suggests the need for the complete wisdom of God, for that insight which comes not solely from our own research, but also from the vehicle of God's wisdom, the teaching Church.

The Christian undergraduate must avoid the two extremes of the a-intellectual pose of the pietistic and the agnosticism of the self-wise inquirer. He must reject the notion that merely because he doesn't fully comprehend, it must not be true. The Christian undergraduate, in short, would do well to ponder Paul's words: "How rich are the depths of God."

Now we are seeing a dim reflection in a mirror;
but then we shall be seeing face to face.
The knowledge that I have now is imperfect; but then
I shall know as fully as I am known [1 Corinthians 13:12].

BELIEVING IS SEEING

THE ADAGE "Seeing is believing" may in human
matters be a somewhat valid guide, but in matters
of divine faith such a catchphrase surely can mis-
lead. In fact, in matters of divine faith the very opposite is often closer to the truth: "Believing is
seeing." If the people had first believed in Jesus the
God-Man, they might have experienced less trouble
in comprehending who he was. They might have
understood more clearly the source of his power and
the significance of his teaching. Even when one be-

lieves, however, he still does not see clearly; but he comprehends, as St. Paul suggests to the Corinthians, darkly as in a mirror.

The central question of our faith, "Who and what is Jesus and his Church to us?" is as pertinent to our contemporary world as it was to the people who saw Jesus in person. More concretely, the question can come down to this: "Do we see Jesus and his Church as they are, or as we want them to be? Do we fashion our own Jesus in our imagination? Do we make our own Church in our own emotional lives? Do we see his Church—teaching, governing, and sanctifying—as the historical extension of Jesus? And do we accept this Church as it is, this assembly of persons, made up of young and old, liberal and conservative, each with his own personal differences, his own faults, foibles, eccentricities, virtues, and vices?"

Sometimes a Christian selects not the complete teaching of Jesus and his Church but rather what he finds suitable to his own personal taste and disposition: a special devotion, a certain moral posture, a particular ascetical practice. Such a Christian seems to look on faith the way some men look on clothes or the grooming of one's hair. There are a variety of styles in these matters, and a man is free to choose what suits him best. In fact, we may be surprised at the variety of styles that are available to us. I recall once at Penn State University pausing before a barbershop to read a list of haircuts available to the undergraduate. The list was rather imposing: sculptor cut; contour; English; all-around; New Yorker; continental; engineer; convertible; twist; Ivy League; crew cut; flattop; Madison Avenue; Florentine; celebrity cut; baron; professional.

Now although these choices of style are available when it comes to grooming one's hair, the same situation does not prevail in matters of faith. Faith does not depend on my own personality and the style that suits me best. Take the individual who considers his devotion to the five holy wounds of Jesus as the very essence of Christianity, but who remains totally mute during the official communal worship of God at the sacrifice of the Mass. One may well wonder if such a Christian really accepts what the Church wishes, or just what he feels is personally satisfying. For if we select only what is personally satisfying about Christianity, we are hardly firm believers. Faith challenges personal whim and personal feeling.

Christians, in electing to follow only the specific moral doctrines they like, are rejecting the Church as teacher. Too many Catholics may be most conscientious about assisting at Mass on Sunday and receiving the Eucharist with great devotion, but they would not hesitate to join a movement against Negroes moving into their neighborhood. A Christian parent may take pains to see that his children receive catechetical instruction, and then be far less eager to see them develop their intellects in science, literature, history, and the arts—advancing as his reason that the only thing that really matters is saving one's soul, and overlooking the fact that the soul's salvation also involves using the God-given gift of intellect which must be developed through work and study.

Christians who select only what they like about the faith may be intellectually lazy. They betray their sloth in glib phrases and in labels which they very cavalierly attach to people and movements. The NAACP is a communist front; all Puerto Ricans are anarchists; all student councils are self-centered. The beauty of such glib generalizations is that they make the situation marvelously simple. The difficulty is that truth is not well served by them, for we see only what we want to see when we fail to consider the whole picture. Seeing what we want to see, believing what we personally want to believe, militates against the Christian attitude toward faith. We are constantly seeing things not as they are, but as we are.

People in personal contact with Jesus saw the Jesus they wanted to see. They did not believe in him and in his claims because they saw only what they wanted. Unwilling to accept him as Messiah, unwilling to investigate his claims, they easily attached a label to his work: "He casts out devils in the name of Satan." They saw what they wanted to see because Jesus had not come according to their image of a Messiah. Their difficulty was not with their eyes; they saw very clearly. It was their minds that were closed; they lived in a world of personal sensibility.

Today it is quite possible that some Catholics believe only what they want to believe, not what Jesus and his Church teaches. Man tends to see faith and morality as he wants to see them, not as they are. An article in *America* noted an interesting experiment conducted among labor and management that illustrates this human factor, an experiment discussed by Alfred Marrow in his book *Making Management Human.* In this experiment, members of management were separated into two groups. Each group was shown a picture. The picture was of a normal man, with little expression on his face. The managers were told the man was forty-six years of age, married, healthy, and successful in his work. One group of managers was told this man was a plant manager; the other group of managers was told the man was a union official.

The group of managers who were told that the man was a union official noted these characteristics: fifty-eight percent found him aggressive; sixty percent found him argumentative; fifty-eight percent found him opinionated; fifty-eight percent found him outspoken. The other group of managers who were told that the man was a plant manager reacted differently. Only eighteen percent found him aggressive; only eight percent found him argumentative; only ten percent found him opinionated; only five percent found him outspoken. Mr. Marrow notes that the same bias was observed among the members of organized labor who took the test. The point is not that labor and management each has its prejudices, but rather that man in general tends to see things as he wants to see them.

The Christian attitude toward faith demands that we look at things through the eyes of Jesus and his Church, not through our own subjective vision. Admittedly, this is a most difficult task. In science we see and consequently we know. In faith we believe, but we never fully comprehend. It is unwise to superimpose the critical apparatus of one discipline upon another. Science is not literary criticism; science is not revelation. They may complement each other, but they are separate and distinct. To say, then, that unless I actually see I will not believe denies the very fundamental attitude required of faith, for faith demands that we believe without full comprehension.

Seeing is not believing, not only because seeing gives knowledge and comprehension whereas faith may not supply comprehension, but also because we tend to see things as we want to see them. In faith, we move out of the world of personal imagination to a transcendent element that is more objective than our own personal attachments. In science, we rely on our own observation of clearly comprehended data; in literature, we rely on personal apprehension of verbal nuance; in faith we rely on the word of another, in divine matters on a revealing God whom we do not see, but in whom we believe. Once we believe, we can begin to see.

80

Now faith is the substance of things to be hoped for,
the evidence of things that are not seen [Hebrews 11:1].

FAITH AND CERTITUDE

IN THE LETTER to the Hebrews, the author describes divine faith as "the substance of things to be
hoped for, the evidence of things not seen," that is,
faith is the basis of certitude for things we do not
comprehend, yet believe. Faith differs from other
intelligent procedures in that it is a venture into the
dark. Despite this misty element, faith is nevertheless not merely a bodily rumbling, not something
felt along the heart. Faith is an intelligent reality,
even though it is not entirely intellectual.

81

Contemporary man encounters intellectual difficulties with faith because science has so conditioned the modern intellect that any observation unverified by science is classified as naïve, ridiculous, silly, perhaps even downright stupid. Man comprehends this rational approach. After all, the knowledge and the certitude presented by science is complete, clear, and experimentally verifiable. Contrast this situation with the scant, dim knowledge offered by faith, and man is inclined to conclude, "Ah, since there is greater knowledge in science than in faith, there must also be greater certitude in science." Herein lies a subtle fallacy. For the certitude of faith differs entirely from the certitude of science.

Knowledge and certitude are not the same thing, and in any discussion of faith the two must be kept separate and distinct. A student requires complete knowledge from mathematics or from experimental sciences because only through complete knowledge will he have certitude. The certitude of faith, however, arises neither from knowledge gained through intuition nor through demonstrative reasoning. Faith agrees with both intuition and demonstration inasmuch as faith gives perfect certitude; faith differs from them in that faith does not give complete knowledge.

Whence arises, then, this certitude given by faith if not from the knowledge faith gives. Man has certitude in faith because the motive for his belief is the unseen, mysterious, revealing God, who cannot be deceived, who does not deceive. A Catholic may say, "I believe because the Church tells me to believe," but this statement is misleading. The motive for a man's divine faith is not the Church; the motive for divine faith is God himself. The Church is God's chosen vehicle through which God informs his people what to believe. The Church is the organ of revelation; it is not the motive for belief.

This motive has historical roots. Quite simply, a man accepts a God who has revealed himself so that man may believe in him. The fundamental revelation is contained in the Old Testament. The fulfillment of the revelation is found in the New Testament, and in these documents we read that Jesus of Nazareth founded an assembly of believers, that he himself selected certain men to lead this group. Historical tradition since the time of Jesus reinforces the view that Jesus intended the leaders of the assembly to be both teachers and legislators in matters of doctrine, and the assembly accepted this situation. Today this assembly is known as the Church, the people of God.

The Church, then, is not the motive for divine faith, but is God's spokesman in history. Since the motive for faith is the revealing God, and since this revealing God has established the means for teaching and directing the members of the Church, a person accepts that teaching and those directions of the Church in the spirit of faith, understanding that this teaching and this legislation is what God wants at this time in history. One may neither fully comprehend nor be rationally convinced of a teaching or a legislation of the Church but, if he truly believes, he accepts it in the spirit of faith because the Church is God's chosen vehicle of revelation.

What impedes our faith in God is our experience with human faith, with faith in man. We may take as certain the opinion or the statement of another; our motive for accepting this statement is the man himself. We have faith in him. A handicapper says, "I've got a hot horse going at Belmont tomorrow in the fifth race. Can't miss." Since this man is experienced in such affairs, you decide to follow his advice and you wager a few bob on that horse. The horse loses. You have lost some money, but you have also lost faith in that man. Human faith is a gambling affair.

If a faculty member predicts that the college eleven will lose more football games than it will win, you may accept this opinion on faith because you know him to be a serious student of the game. When the team wins more than it loses, your faith in this man is shattered. In human faith, we just do not have certitude because our motive is man, not the revealing God.

Each time one crosses the street at a busy intersection, he believes that motorists will stop at the red light—but still one lacks certitude about this. A person told by an airline that the aircraft is the newest available would lose faith in that airline if, upon boarding the aircraft, he found Lindbergh's lunch on the seat. You're not surprised, if a man on the street corner offers you an original Michelangelo painting, to find that a calendar is attached.

Clearly, man is conned by other men, and consequently our tendency to accept things on human faith is diminished. Because our faith in man is often shaken, we tend to consider that any faith—even divine faith—is risky and suspect. And this is particularly true when the chosen vehicle of God's revelation, the Church, is constituted by other men.

Our motive for divine faith, however, is the revealing God. We should not make the mistake of judging faith by our feelings of satisfaction or depression. A person would be foolish to say, "I believe, and all I've got is problems." He is like the man who believes in Yoga and ends up with arthritis. Such a situation is irrelevant to the certitude of faith. We are certain neither because we have complete knowledge nor because faith makes us feel good nor even because of the Church as such; but because the source of the revelation is ultimately God himself.

The certitude of faith deepens as man becomes more attuned to God, the motive for belief. Man must, however, realize that even after his faith is strengthened, he may still lack a totally satisfying knowledge. It is quite possible that the more he studies faith, the more difficulties he encounters with faith. Faith ever remains a venture into darkness, yet a venture that is not unintelligent because the reason for faith is the revealing God. We do not fully comprehend, but we ought to realize the validity of those words: "Faith is the substance of things to be hoped for, the evidence of things not seen."

Therefore let him who thinks he stands
take heed lest he fall [1 Corinthians 10:12].

THINKING WITH THE CHURCH

AN INTERESTING, but little known work of Ignatius
Loyola is entitled "Rules for Thinking with the
Church." Not only are these rules eminently practical in themselves, but they seem particularly appropriate today when institutionalized Christianity
is being challenged.

Ignatius Loyola was, even before he was founder
of the Society of Jesus, a man strongly dedicated to
the Church. He considered that his followers would
be especially conspicuous by their devotion to the

Church and its work in the world, particularly through the education of people. Ignatius may not have foreseen Georgetown, Fordham, Xavier, Holy Cross, his namesake Loyolas, and the other college campuses directed by Jesuits throughout the United States today, but he did desire that his followers be ever intent upon bringing the witness of the Church to the people and to the culture where his followers would be working.

Ignatius always urged the view that the Church was the great witness to Jesus, the extension of Jesus in this world. His Jesuits were to defend and to explain the Church, her teachings and her decisions, to the world. The Jesuits were to teach the truths of Christianity and their practical applications in various nations and among different peoples. In all events, in all dealings, in all discussions, in every debate about means of adapting Christianity, in every dispute about the proper application of Christian principles, the exact teaching of the Church served as a guide. For this purpose Ignatius set down what he called "Rules for Thinking with the Church."

Loyola's "Rules for Thinking with the Church" have a scriptural basis, one source of which is Paul's letter to the people of Corinth. The parallels between the situation that confronted Paul in A.D. 51 and the situation that confronts us in our own day and age are striking.

The historical background of Paul's letter to the people of Corinth reveals its contemporary significance. After Paul left Corinth, some Christian converts from Judaism, who once had been most zealous in their practice of Christianity, arrived there. These people apparently tolerated a great laxity in the relations between the new Christians and the pagans of that day. Their presence and their teaching lowered the whole spiritual level of a promising Church. Paul heard disturbing reports about the work of these people, whom he called the "false apostles." So Paul's letter to the people of Corinth contains advice to the Christians about their attitude toward such false apostles and their relationships with the pagans they encountered.

In the tenth chapter of this letter Paul recalls examples from the Old Testament, specifically the Book of Exodus. And he points out rather clearly the presumption of the chosen people of Israel when they reverted to pagan rites, such as dancing before the golden calf, and engaged in all kinds of licentious activity more proper to paganism than to the worship of the one, true God.

Paul reminds the people of Corinth that they are not to err as did the chosen people, that they are never to be presumptuous; that is, they are never to think that merely because they are baptized Christians and believe in God and nominally follow Christ, they can then do whatever they feel inclined to do in the name of righteousness or so-called personal freedom. Paul reminds the Corinthians that there is a definite Christian way of life, and that this life is incompatible with the paganism of the day.

"He who thinks himself to be standing easily," Paul reminds the Corinthians, "let him take care lest he fall." The Christian takes such care by thinking with the teachings of Jesus, the teachings of Paul, the teachings of the Church. What Ignatius Loyola proposes in his "Rules for Thinking with the Church" is not unlike what Paul insists on for the early Church at Corinth.

Paul's words to the Corinthians, and Ignatius' teaching regarding the Church and her members, have relevance today. Yet the existing situation, no matter how analogous to Paul's day, is different. The dangers for the Christian today are far more subtle, far more intangible, yet nonetheless real. Dancing before the golden calf is an overt pagan practice to which most undergraduates are not tempted. But it is quite possible that Christian undergraduates follow the standards of today's pagans by adopting either an immoral or an amoral view of life.

Living as we do in close proximity and on a friendly basis with others who are either lapsed Catholics, non-Catholics, or anti-Catholics, and finding such people to be enjoyable company and rather jolly folk, it is very easy to transfer their religious attitude to ourselves. We find ourselves approving what these people approve. We may find ourselves opposed to civil rights for all people; we may find ourselves supporting the Playboy Club; we may find ourselves indiscriminately reading books and magazines that exploit a lurid sensuality; ultimately we may find ourselves seriously questioning the Church's right to speak to us about our own personal morality and our own personal religious beliefs.

The false apostles today may not appear as distinct individuals exhorting us to adopt a pagan way of life. The false apostles today may very well be the society and the community in which we live, a society and a community that may or may not pay even a lip service to God and that is in many ways hostile to a teaching Church. Now we cannot very easily divorce ourselves from our society or our community; we must live in these circumstances. If we have a country where the name of God may not legally be mentioned in classrooms supported by the state, then the Christian must be strong enough to live in this world as a Christian and not be influenced morally by such a society. It is the price the American Christian pays for social pluralism. He is friendly and charitable to those unsympathetic to his religious convictions, but he does not follow such acquaintances in moral and religious practices and beliefs.

Today, when a renewed emphasis on free speech has prompted people to speak their mind on every subject, it is especially imperative that the Christian undergraduate heed the voice of the teaching Church in matters of faith and morality. In an age when mass communication shows little discrimination in matters theological, it is especially necessary for the Christian to recognize the half-truths of superficial reportage in the secular press, on radio and

90

television. At a time when people are being urged to express themselves more freely, it is most important that the Christian know clearly what the Church says. And the source for this is the Church's document, not the report of the Associated Press nor the ideas of the merely nominal Catholic down the street.

Some people who pride themselves on their independent moral views believe that they are actually avant-garde, ahead of the Church, when in reality they may be merely out of step with the Church. The line drawn between those in advance of the Church and those out of step is generally a very thin one, and the average Christian is at a loss to distinguish. Such people are like the lady in the congregation who always kept getting ahead of the others during the recitation of the hymns and psalms in the service. One day after the congregation had recited the twenty-second Psalm, another member of the congregation was heard to mutter: "How did she get to the still waters while the rest of us were lying down in green pastures?" The lady may have thought she was right, that she was really in advance of the others, whereas actually she was only failing to stay joined to the group.

The warning of Paul to the presumptuous, to the nominal Christian, rings clear today: "Let the one who thinks he is standing firm be careful lest he fall." One might paraphrase by adding, "And let the one who thinks he is ahead of the times take care lest he be found to be simply out of step."

So I bear it all for the sake of those who are chosen,
so that in the end they may have the
salvation that is in Christ Jesus and the
eternal glory that comes with it [2 Timothy 2:10].

MY CHURCH HAS

AN UNLISTED NUMBER

SHOULD AMERICAN RELIGION of the purely private type ever enter the public domain, it may well resemble the half-time show presented yesterday at East Lansing, Michigan. The musical subject was religion. Such theological gems as "People," "Let's Get Together," and "Put Your Hand in the Hand of the Man" formed the core of the hymns. During the playing of "Put Your Hand in the Hand of the Man," the crowd clapped and rocked in an abortive effort at unison with the band. A petite Michigan

92

cheerleader, obviously chosen for qualities other than rhythm, clapped and stomped as if the song's beat were iambic, though the lyrics clearly scan according to an anapestic meter. The pathos of her struggle was moving, but like many a figure in American fiction she was oblivious to the contrapuntal effect she was achieving.

A most moving segment of the performance was an arrangement that merged the world of sport with the Jesus world; against a muted playing of the Michigan fight song, "Hail to the Victors Valiant," the band played the theme from *Jesus Christ, Superstar*. The resultant pastiche symbolized that native blend of religion and sport, that type of muscular Christianity indigenous to America, in which the halfback presumably makes the most likely candidate for canonization. While listening and watching, I thought of other combinations for such half-time shows. It struck me that here at Xavier the band might play a muted "Xavier for Aye" as a background for the hymn "Nearer, My God, to Thee"— since no college football team comes weekly closer to annihilation than the Musketeers.

This American approach to religion through muscle, through sport, through visceral experience, through pop music, through half-time shows, through moral imperatives from sportscasters— echoes of ancient fertility cults during which man was stressed and God overlooked—all reveal the American attitude that church membership and the sacramental life are ultimately unnecessary. Just feel, man, and believe; man, tune in Jesus; that's where it's at; boy, wow, gee, yeah, yeah, yeah, ain't it good to go with Jesus? One of the ironies in our Age of Aquarius is that I am asked to reject ecclesiastical propositions on the grounds of irrelevance, but I am asked to shriek and jump and clap with the semiarticulate members of the now generation who are hardly capable of a complete sentence, and whose main mode of emphasis relies on vocal repetition of the same old fragments. Knowledge isn't deepened; insight isn't reached; only the volume is turned up. I'm all for going with the Jesus of Scripture; I have doubts about the Jesus of Simon and Garfunkel or of Bob Dylan or of Webber and Rice.

If I want to go with Jesus, I prefer to follow what Paul says in his letters to Timothy. Prior to the maxims recorded in chapter two, verse 11 of the second letter to Timothy, Paul says very simply that "salvation . . . is in Christ Jesus." To avoid isolating this passage from Paul's context in these letters to Timothy, read this section against the background of the first letter to Timothy, chapter three, verses 14-15, where Paul writes: "I wanted you to know how people ought to behave in God's family—that is, in the Church of the living God, which upholds the truth and keeps it safe." Jesus and the Church are so identified in Paul's mind that one cannot be had without the other.

Our world unfolds in many ways a standard of values that can only be called ridiculous. Consider the cultural inversion that occurs. Arnell's Country

Club in Walill, New York, charges only $19.50 a day, meals included. Rather inexpensive, until you realize that this country club caters exclusively to dogs. Some clients worry so about their pets that they provide the operators of the club with raincoats for their dogs, begging them to see to it their pooches are covered when it rains. I wonder why they don't realize that most dogs know enough to come in out of the rain?

Or have you kept up with the speeches in Congress recently? Consider the following in the light of the burning issues that confront the republic. Senator Harry Byrd of Virginia and Representative John Rarick of Louisiana both delivered impassioned pleas against the federal court's banning of the playing of "Dixie" in Alabama. Representative Jack Kemp of upstate New York introduced legislation making April 30 "Pledge-of-Allegiance-to-Our-Flag-Day." He allowed as how this brilliant idea arose from the third-grade class of Cleveland Hill School, Cheektowaga, New York. Representative Clarence Miller of Ohio urged that we all take greater pride in America's accomplishments, which he found exemplified in the exciting statistic that the United States has six times the total road mileage of the Soviet Union and twelve and one-half times the surfaced-road mileage. They used to compare bathtubs and radios. Representative William Jennings Bryan Dorn of South Carolina declared, "I am shocked and amazed that a professional football game was broadcast nationwide on September 5, at a time when thousands of high-school football teams were opening the season." If he was "shocked and amazed" at that, imagine his response to Vietnam, My Lai, Attica, and Watts. Wonder what he would have said had he been with Lee at Appomattox? Representative Fred Rooney of Pennsylvania admitted to "particular pride in the fact that a very famous musical instrument maker is located in my congressional district. The selection of the Allen organ used at the opening of the John F. Kennedy Center is certainly noteworthy." Funny, nobody else seemed to note it.

If one desires to know why Americans reject church membership and a sacramental system and a teaching Church; if anyone wants to learn what prompts Americans to create their own religions, just read the newspapers. Better, read the *Congressional Record*. Literally an absurd world where there are no principles except self. A world suffering moral crises, and our leaders are concerned about high-school football, the pledge of allegiance, the name of an organ, and interstate highways. I had better not lump the playing of "Dixie" with these other absurdities, since I have been told on good authority that Moses received those lyrics shortly after he received the decalogue.

Today is the day of the guru. If you find your own guru, you don't need a teaching Church. But perhaps some disenchantment has set in with the advice available from gurus. A recent cartoon showed an American atop a mountain with his guru sitting on a prayer rug, and it was captioned: "I travel all the way from Chillicothe, and your only advice is 'Keep your options open'?"

There is indeed today that tendency to play coy, to be tactful, to avoid confrontation. In certain cases, though, these are merely euphemisms for avoiding the truth. Teachers, for example, as Cleveland Amory recorded recently in the *Saturday Review*, are adept at circumlocutions which, if they do not exactly deceive, at least avoid the issue. They tell a parent: "John's social adjustment has been less than satisfactory." Translated this means that the kids all hate John. Or the teacher says, "Debbie is overly interested in the work of other children," that is, Debbie cheats in school. Again, "Bruce tends not to respect the property of others." Righto, Bruce steals whatever isn't nailed down. Or "Jane is exceptional in her social maturity," which means that Jane is the only girl in the fifth grade with pierced ears and eye shadow. The tactful soul and the con man could sometimes belong to the same club.

Finally, and I repeat myself, there is abroad today the idea that whatever is new is by that very fact superior to whatever is old. During the "Race of the Week" yesterday, the announcer interviewed a young trainer, one of the under-thirty variety. The announcer asked the young man if his technique differed from that of the late great "Sunny Jim" Fitzsimmons. "Oh yes," declared the confident young trainer. "You see, Mr. Fitz belonged to the old school, the hard-line school. I treat each of my horses as an individual." Personalism, my friends, has entered the world of the turf, one of the last bastions of absolutes. All the old principles are crumbling: never bet on a race for two-year-old maidens; never bet on a filly in an allowance race with colts; never bet a long shot to show. The world indeed is changing.

My point, however, is simply that the young man is only *different* from Mr. Fitz or Ben Jones or Eddie Neloy or any of the great trainers of the past thirty years. Thus far he's not as good as any of them, hardly superior to them. He's just different from them. And mere difference doesn't prove superiority. By parallel, if my own private religion differs from the Church of Jesus Christ, it is not thereby better. My new religion has lotsa feeling, lotsa gutsy reactions, but no moral code and no dogma, no ritual, and no sacraments. It's simpler, but can I thereby argue that it must be closer to the simple life of Jesus?

Culture does affect religion. And American absurdity in the Age of Aquarius can subtly influence our thinking about the Church founded by Jesus. If we want to create our own religion, however, then before we start calling it authentically Christian, we ought to try to square it with Scripture. I'm suggesting that a good start might be made by comparing this new religious attitude today with Paul's letters to Timothy, where the Church, with its teachings and its moral codes, is not only valid but necessary, in Paul's view, for truth and wisdom.

They are destined to be lost. They make foods into
their god and they are proudest of something
they ought to think shameful; the things they
think important are earthly things [Philippians 3:19].

THE CHRISTIAN RITUALIST

IF RELIGION is your God, then it may be that God
is not fully in your religion. Ritual without an appreciation of its significance is easily practiced, and
some Catholics prove this every Sunday at Mass. In
his letter to the people of Philippi, St. Paul stresses
the stupidity of ritualists who have made dietary
laws and external rites their God.

For these ritualists, God resembles an ethereal
Santa Claus dispensing spiritual goodies—and in
some cases material goodies as well—to all the duti-
ful children. For some ritualists, God uses human

lives as dice and his hand is thus observed in every natural disaster like an earthquake or an avalanche. When the ritualist is delivered from these catastrophes, he reasons that God must be pleased with his observance.

There has developed among some Catholics the belief that God, no matter how a person lives his moral life, remains on that person's side as long as he performs the proper ritual. For many years, as long as the ritualist abstained from meat on Friday, God was pleased. Whether his abstinence was properly motivated did not enter into consideration. The really important fact was that he abstain, not why he abstained. Similarly, a most necessary detail in the ritualist's weekly calendar was going to Mass on Sunday. Literally, he went to Mass; he was there. The ritual may have been meaningless to him; he may never have comprehended the symbolic significance of group worship. He did not really assist at Mass; he just went to Mass. He had performed for another week, and God was pleased. That there is significance in the official worship of the Church and a relationship between his assistance at Mass and his daily life and social attitudes eluded the ritualist.

Some Catholic ritualists even believe that an abundance of material goods is due, at least partially, to their ritualistic fidelity. That these gifts are not shared by less fortunate people simply indicates that the poor have failed to please God by the proper ritual. That the gifts gained by the ritualist may have been obtained unjustly or dishonestly matters little. After all, God helps those who help themselves. He has performed his ritual, and God can't help but be satisfied. As for the more unfortunate people, let them work as hard as the ritualist works, and they will obtain God's blessing through material goods. Unless these less fortunate souls fail to observe the proper ritual into the bargain.

The Catholic ritualist's commitment is hardly to the teaching of Jesus Christ, but rather to a type of ritual in which the entire world must join if it wishes to be saved. Worship the right idols, worship the true God, and all will be well. Such a procedure is as self-defeating as it is mechanical. It is the attitude of the immature and the unintelligent.

Catholics now must be more mature about their religion and their ritual. They must learn to live in a way that reflects their unity during the worship of God at Mass. Catholics are urged, not coerced, to abstain from meat on Friday in the spirit of self-denial. Catholics are asked to cease being spectators at a ritual and to share more fully in the sacrificial offering and in the Eucharistic Communion. Catholics are asked to observe the relevance of the law of justice and charity in their dealings with all men, to realize that joining with others at Mass symbolizes the unity of love with men in our daily lives in Christ, through Christ, and with Christ. Catholics share together at the communion table in a manner that is to do more than merely symbolize their union with others at work and at play.

Yet the ritualists remain among us. They are found in all religions, because they have turned religion into God. They belong to a denomination for the wrong reasons. Opportunists to the core, these ritualists believe that if you merely join the proper church and say the magic words, all will be well between you and God. Such ritualists are for all the world like politicians making campaign speeches, whose purpose is simply to identify with the group in order to gain their votes. The candidate was hardly interested in the worship of God when he declared: "My great-grandfather was an Episcopalian (stony silence from the crowd), but my great-grandmother belonged to the Congregational Church (still silence). My grandfather was a Baptist (more silence), but my grandmother was a Presbyterian (still a frigid silence). But I had a great-aunt who was a Methodist (loud and enthusiastic applause), and I am here to declare that I have always followed the religion of my great-aunt (loud and continued cheering)." He was using religion in much the same way the ritualist uses his religion: solely to be in the acceptable organization. For the ritualist feels that if he has properly allied himself to an institution, then God will bless him. It is solely a matter of externals.

Today, Catholics enjoy a greater freedom and a greater responsibility. A freedom to make their moral choices, a responsibility to act in accord with their proper moral judgments. Some Catholics may continue to find comfort in the ritualistic pattern;

they will hang on. Others will find this new freedom disconcerting and unsettling; they will feel that the Church no longer stands for anything and will sever their relationship with the Church. Others will realize that there are two important aspects in their relationship with God and men. One is worship of God, the other is proper moral living. Both are necessary. For moral living without the sacramental and sacrificial union with Christ is mere humanitarianism. Worship without moral living is simply ritualism. Religion without God is pantheism; God without religion is infidelity. Both God and religion are important.

St. Paul clearly reminds man that some have turned ritualism into a God, whereas a ceremony is a means to reach God. There is certainly a need for Christians to grow more aware of their unity, more aware of the need to live moral lives consistent with that love which is the central force behind the sacrifice they offer.

Sing the words and tunes of the psalms and hymns
when you are together, and go on singing and
chanting to the Lord in your hearts, so that always and
everywhere you are giving thanks to God who is our Father
in the name of our Lord Jesus Christ [Ephesians 5:19-20].

WORSHIP:

GIVING AND RECEIVING

IN HIS LETTER to the people of Ephesus, St. Paul
summarizes what the Christian does at the sacrifice
of the Mass: He gives praise to God and he gives
thanks to God. Man's activity at Mass must be dynamic; he cannot be passive and still claim to have
participated in the sacrifice of the Mass. Largely
because of a failure to comprehend the Mass, however, Christians do not always appreciate what they
are actually doing when they assist at the sacrifice.
So a Christian would do well to consider on occa-

sion exactly what the Mass is and what his part in the Mass should be.

Three doctrinal truisms regarding the sacrifice of the Mass offer matter for reflection. First, the sacrifice of the Mass is the central act of our worship of God; second, the Mass is both a sacrifice and a sacrament; third, the Mass has value for us as the representation of Jesus' own sacrifice of his life on the cross. These ideas we know; these ideas we as Christians accept.

But for many priests and laymen there are psychological problems connected with the Mass even though we know, dogmatically, what the Mass is. One of these psychological problems is exemplified by the person who says quite honestly: "I get nothing from the Mass," or "The Mass is meaningless to me," or "I merely go 'cause I guess it would be a serious offense against God not to—at least I've been told this, and I suppose I believe it." The solution to this psychological problem lies, I think, in understanding fundamentally what the Mass is.

The Mass is our official public central act of worship. Jesus instituted it; the Church sustains it. Jesus was the first to offer the Mass; the priests in history have continued to offer it in his name. To comprehend the Mass, one must first appreciate that it is this official public central act of worship.

As with other public events in our lives, however, the Mass can easily become routine. Or it may become so official that it doesn't reach us. Thus, it is necessary to move from a consideration of this official function of the Mass to the consideration that it is both a sacrifice and a sacrament.

Since the Mass is a sacrifice, it means that we must offer ourselves, we must give ourselves. The Mass is a giving, an offering, a sacrifice. The Mass is also a sacrament, the Eucharist, and this means a sharing, a receiving. Both aspects of sacrament and sacrifice must be present for full and complete participation in the Mass. The sacrifice without the sacrament is incomplete; the sacrament without the sacrifice is superstitious. Yet some consider mere attendance at the sacrifice as sufficient for supernatural growth, while others consider reception of the sacrament as superseding the sacrifice. For completeness, however, both sacrament and sacrifice are necessary; there must be both a giving and a sharing. Perhaps those who fail to "get anything from Mass" are not really giving anything at Mass, and thus they have eliminated a necessary prerequisite for sacrifice.

Another psychological problem with the Mass is that it is a symbolic act. To comprehend the Mass one must penetrate the symbol. There are conventions in the offering of the Mass. At certain times we rise; for example, to hear the good news, to profess our faith, to recite the Our Father. At other times we are seated. At other times we kneel. Yet even these rubrics are not absolute. In some countries the congregation stands throughout the entire Mass; for them the gesture is more respectful, in keeping with their cultural traditions.

106

Now the conventions of the Mass must be understood, just as the conventions of any sport must be understood. In rugby, for example, the action is continuous. "Wouldn't it be more efficient for them to huddle?" asks an American. And the Englishman seeing American football asks, "Wouldn't the game be more spontaneous if the action were sustained?" The two games are different, and to understand the game, the conventions must be understood. Likewise, to appreciate the Mass, the symbolic format must be understood.

The basic structure of the Mass is a meal, a form Jesus chose at the Last Supper. One of our problems with the symbol, perhaps, may be that the family meal has lost its significance. The TV dinner has helped to eliminate this aspect of daily domestic life, and the automobile has enabled younger family members to excuse themselves before dessert to get back on the road. The loss of the family meal is just one of the unfortunate results of many changes in family life. Indeed, family life has itself changed in structure and in its traditional meaning. And if we have lost the sense of family and the idea of a family meal, we admittedly are going to have difficulty understanding the symbol of the Mass, which is that of a community meal.

Jesus chose this form because it was meaningful to the people of his time. Our comprehension of this symbol is less the fault of the symbol than of our own inattention. Often we simply do not care to be bothered to try to understand. Man tends not to

107

hear if he does not want to. A child pretends not to hear his mother calling him because he wishes to continue what he is doing. Yet he can hear the faintest tinkle of the bell that signals the arrival of the ice-cream man. Children hear what they want to hear, and so do Christians. We could comprehend the symbols of the Mass if only we were concerned enough with God to attend to his worship.

Some accidental aspects of the Mass, of course, may impede our understanding and appreciation of this central symbol. The huge churches where Mass is offered are not conducive to community (let alone family) feelings; the ancient vestments worn by the priest can present a psychological barrier to some; the shocking forms of statuary stationed strategically throughout some churches distract from the sacrifice and cater to a maudlin type of piety. Maybe, then, we Christians need to find new symbolic forms to aid us in achieving the spirit of the form Jesus chose. Perhaps every age will.

Some points that strike me as helpful even in our present situation would include the following: Less pretentious church buildings, particularly in matter of size; not every pastor need build a basilica to his memory. Why not have churches so constructed that the people are not more than a relatively few feet from the altar? Or better yet, Mass could be celebrated in private homes and apartments where a neighborhood group might gather. The Last Supper was held in the upper room. Priests ought to be so mobile they can offer Mass at several neighborhood stations throughout the week for people in their parishes. Perhaps, too, the obligation to assist at Mass could be extended so the obligation might be fulfilled on any day of the week, not necessarily on Sunday. More Masses ought to be celebrated in the evening—as was the Last Supper—and at night when the entire family could conveniently worship together. Maybe, when laymen assume more of the duties of conducting the external affairs of the parish, priests will be more free to give themselves to more frequent celebration of the Mass on days during the week.

Sometimes any new departure in ritual shocks us as vulgar or unaesthetic. And I would agree. Vulgar in the root meaning of the word, something common; the sacrifice is not a vulgar thing, but its format may be common—that is, for all. As for the aesthetic aspect of the Mass, there was nothing very aesthetic about either the Crucifixion or the Last Supper, even if artists have stylized re-creations of both events. The Mass commemorates a very earthy, a very human event.

Until a new form appears, however, we live with our present improved version. We must remember that at Mass we are first of all giving, then receiving. The church building is not a spiritual comfort station or a rest area where we come for sustenance; it is a place where we offer ourselves—our successes and our failures, our disappointments and our joys— to God. It is a place where we share with others by joining them in communal worship.

A Christian must overcome any thinking that has been conditioned by casuists who tell us our obligation is fulfilled if we are physically present. Just being among the Alka-Seltzer crowd ringing the rear of the church at the 12:30 Mass may satisfy our obligation; it hardly profits our souls. There is more to Mass than simple attendance. We must enter into this central act of worship, offering ourselves not statically and individually, but dynamically and as a unit, as we give praise due to our Lord and our God, as we give to him, and through him to others, our most precious possession—ourselves.

When Pentecost day came round, they had all met in
one room, when suddenly they heard what sounded like a
powerful wind from heaven, the noise of which filled the
entire house in which they were sitting; and something
appeared to them that seemed like tongues of fire; these
separated and came to rest on the head of each of them.
They were all filled with the Holy Spirit, and
began to speak foreign languages as the
Spirit gave them the gift of speech [Acts 2:1-4].

UP AGAINST THE WALL,
MOTHER CHURCH

THE EARLY CHRISTIAN community, the beginnings
of the Church, differed considerably from what we
know today, if we accept Luke's account in the Acts
of the Apostles. The early Christians were largely a
gathering of witnesses committed to Jesus and sensitive to the inspiration of the Holy Spirit. The chief
dimension of their lives was a mutual sharing that
was religiously symbolized in the Eucharist. This
early Church satisfied man's social needs, since she
enabled him to give himself to his neighbor. It satis-

fied his need to bind himself, since he was committed to the person of Jesus. It satisfied his need for transcendence, since he experienced the inspiration of the Holy Spirit.

History wrought dramatic changes in the Church, starting with the Edict of Constantine in A.D. 313. As the Church developed, she gripped herself in a Renaissance authoritarianism from which we have only recently been released by the Second Vatican Council. During the long years of this ecclesiastical development, leaders of the Church occasionally sounded less like Jesus than like Machiavelli. In any event, the impression was created of a rigid, immovable institution that lasted from the sixteenth century until the 1950s.

There still lingers among us a tendency to speak of our religion not as a life of the spirit but rather as a life of defined doctrines, of legislation, of jurisdiction. These elements, necessary as they are, hardly serve as the primary factors of a genuine Christian life-style. The Church has maintained beliefs and encouraged practices, many of which are too easily turned to a self-centered, not a Jesus-centered, religion. Good as these beliefs and practices may be, they do not present the picture of a Christian community such as the one recorded in the Acts of the Apostles.

So a strong reaction to the Church has set in, from James Forman's manifesto for black persons to the absence of young people in sharing in the Eucharist. The Church has neither the power nor the resources of a General Motors, a Procter and Gamble, or an IBM. And because she is vulnerable, she tends to blend comfortably with the existing political system, a factor which, for all its practical accommodations, may lead the Church to compromise herself to gain worldly acceptance. And then, precisely because the Church is a vulnerable institution, the mob may well cry out, "Up against the wall, Mother Church."

In our own reaction to these same developments, we can all too easily confuse our loyalty to the institution with our loyalty to Jesus. But let's remember that the Church is not man's final goal. The Church is the foremost witness of Jesus in this world; she is a vehicle. Since the Church is the witness of Jesus, she must show concern, as did her founder, with total man in the light of Jesus' teaching and under the guidance of the Holy Spirit. We recoil perhaps at such a suggestion because we Anglo-Saxons believe that our positivism will solve all problems. Our life experience, however, reveals that man in his totality remains a mystery which is inexplicable on purely natural and human levels. Man has yearnings within himself that remain unsatisfied by his various lives: political, social, intellectual. His restless soul can be calmed by the word of God.

The Church must increase and intensify her efforts to offer man opportunities for hearing the word of God, for sharing the sacramental life. It is in this area that the priest must be most zealous and eager to serve. The Church and the priest are for

113

man; man is not for the Church and the priest. Likewise, man must be offered a solid understanding of life and of death by the Church. Above all, in her mission to man, the Church must never appear as a computer, storing information and answers for the opportune moment. The Church must ever be a servant attempting to reach all men, but the handing down of edicts and the issuance of pronouncements communicates about as well as does shouting to a deaf-mute.

The Church's image is changing, but perhaps not rapidly enough. Jesus' Church was not as priestly a Church as we possess today. Some ecclesiastics speak as if the main problem confronting the Church is the diminishing number of priests and seminarians. The Church's primary mission, however, is not to maintain a steady flow of candidates for holy orders, important as this is. Emphasizing the priestly segment of the Church tends to frustrate the insights of the laity. Emphasizing the cult of age, which appears to be one qualification for ecclesiastical advancement, serves to stifle the brilliance of the young. No priest has a corner on the Holy Spirit's counsel any more than an older person, merely because of age, possesses richer understanding than a younger person.

The times demand that the Church be more ethically aware. The Church cannot afford the delightful luxury of wrapping herself in what is comfortable, but not necessarily Christian. The early Christians, for example, always spoke about sharing. Today's Christian seems fundamentally concerned with defending private property. At the risk of sounding like a mouthpiece for the Soviets, what is so sacrosanct about private property that it should be considered more basic than the concept of sharing among contemporary Christians?

The Church must return to her roots; she must radicalize herself without the brutalizing effect some radicals achieve when they gain control. Even if we cannot re-create the culture prevalent at the time of the Acts of the Apostles, we could do worse than imitate their spirit.

The Church's main task is to assist man in finding wisdom in the sight of God, which is another way of saying salvation. To do this, the battle cry need not be, "Up against the wall." Pope John's metaphor of opening the Church's windows, rather, seems a far saner approach. There is less reason to put the Church up against the wall than to hold her up to the light, to see her as she ought to be. And the Church must see clearly if she is to root up and to tear down, to build and to plant.

In order for this effort to be effective, Christians must be aware that they are alive in this world at this time in history. The docetist tendency has long affected Christians: that is, we have a tendency to consider religion as if it existed in some disembodied form. We have been unwilling to realize what was most apparent to the early Church: that the Church is earthy, mundane, real, human, vital, alive, concerned with others in their human dimension, without at the same time being wedded to a worldly materialism.

Individual members of the Church have the task of praying and worshiping together, of eagerly sharing, both spiritually and materially, with others, through friendship, through community efforts, through working for a better world. Especially is there a need for a greater spirit of prayer and reflection among us. Our dialogue and interaction will be only as good as the reflection and prayer that precedes it. Communal effort is a mere ritualistic shell.

Pentecost was an experience of the early Church, a profound experience that helped to shape the forms of early Christian attitudes and of communities. But the Holy Spirit did not come then once and for all. He continues to inspire and to illumine, if only man will listen. Part of the Church's task is to listen. For too long the Church and churchmen have pronounced. In a day of ambiguity such as our own, prayerful listening is required if the Spirit is effectively to renew us according to the mind of Jesus Christ.

The whole group of believers was united, heart and soul;
no one claimed for his own use anything that he had,
as everything they owned was held in common [Acts 4:32].

IF YOU'RE OUT OF THE CHURCH,
YOU'RE OUT OF FEAR

A PERSON who is out of the Church ought surely to
be out of fear. Fear is either servile dread or respectful reverence. If a person no longer fears ex-
communication, he leaves the Church; if he loses
his reverence for the institution founded by Jesus,
he leaves the Church. In both cases he is out of
fear; he has lost his fear. And the contemporary
phenomenon of persons, whether fearless or irrev-
erent, who leave the Catholic Church prompts some
thoughts on the identity of the Church.

117

Historically, Protestant Christians have stressed the invisible Church, with emphasis on the Scripture text: "the kingdom of God is within you" (Luke 17:21). The Catholic considers the Church rather as more visible, as an objectively constructed institution with external and juridical machinery. Whether Protestants need more stress on the visible Church is not our problem. We Catholics, however, need a fuller appreciation of the hidden, the invisible Church. The question confronting us is precisely this: Is a faithful Catholic defined solely by visible criteria? Or to put it another way, may a good Catholic remain invisible?

Today's Catholic lives with a hierarchical Church, complete with traditions and defined processes in juridical and liturgical matters. Today's Catholic also possesses a newly realized freedom, partly because of the Second Vatican Council, partly because he is a child of the times. His problem centers on finding a way whereby he can accept the visible teaching Church yet exercise this freedom. The Catholic must be prepared to live with a definite tension in his life. On the one hand, the visible Church; on the other hand, the spirit of freedom within him, the soul of the invisible Church.

A crucial situation arises because, unlike Protestant Christianity, our Catholic ecclesiastical administrators also officially determine theological propriety. While bishops are often not trained theologians, they must make theological decisions. In this day of sensitivity and ambiguity, it would be

118

welcome were the bishops to delegate this authority to trained theologians, but this is hardly likely.

Some Catholics react to this crisis by declaring that the situation is hopeless. They leave the official Church and go underground. They divorce themselves from the visible Church, placing the total stress upon the invisible spirit. And by so doing, they reveal a lack of fear or reverence for the visible Church. Others blindly continue within the structure, pausing neither to question the official Church nor to exercise their freedom. They grow spiritually slothful. They lack a fear or reverence for the invisible Church of the spirit, relying largely on episcopal fiat to defend the theological details of their spiritual lives.

A middle ground appears possible. A person who remains in the visible Church with a healthy respect for the invisible spirit will live of necessity in constant spiritual tension. Yet such tension is not new. It resembles the biblical tension of man's having to live in this world while preparing for the next, or of working for a better universe while fully aware that it is transient. Religious tension is nothing really new for the reflective Christian.

To remain a visible Catholic, as Frederick Sontag suggests in a recent *America* article, one must be in good standing with the prescriptions of the Church's written codes and with the formal decisions based upon them. But can an individual live in the invisible Church by fulfilling the spirit of the law, even if he publicly appears to violate the letter of that

119

law? There is a danger, of course, that the individual who stresses the spirit of the law over the letter may degenerate into a smug and self-righteous individual. But Professor Sontag asks, might not a person conceivably stand forth not as one denying the visible authority of the Church, but rather as one stressing the virtues which the visible Church encourages? The invisible Church might then become visible in acts of mercy and charity, though not in public defense of opinions at variance with the doctrines promulgated by the visible, teaching Church.

I do not mean to suggest that the invisible Church may ever substitute for the public and juridical relationship of the individual to his Church, much less to deny this relationship. The situation is largely a matter of emphasis. Were a person who accepts only the invisible Church of the spirit to insist that the *only* way the Church can reform is to make herself over into his image and likeness, or if he were to deny the visible Church's jurisdiction over him, then he surely would have misplaced the emphasis. In fact, he would be starting his own church.

For centuries, Catholics have long identified their Church with formal pronouncements, public procedures, and visible acts. Today, Professor Sontag says, Catholics may be forced to acknowledge an invisible Church. Yet this acknowledgment is accomplished neither by denying visible authority nor by defying this authority. It is done rather by letting the visible structure stand clearly before us and acknowledging it, without focusing attention on that visible structure. Catholics may have to learn a totally new interior way, a way of tension. Living with such a constant tension between the visible and invisible may be either creative or destructive. One's attitude conditions which it will be.

When a person's total religious life is externalized solely in the Mass, religion is hardly a burden. If, however, the living of one's religious life shifts from ceremonial observance, a whole new interior life may arise. The interior life may never be totally externalized; the spirit cannot be perfectly reflected in any visible structure. God, I would urge, apparently wants us to live between the two, between the visible and the invisible.

Catholics have in the past tended to equate religion with definable truth. In the invisible Church, man knows largely the indisputable and noncontroversial acts of charity, mercy, and justice. So the issue reduces itself to whether the Incarnation of Jesus is basically a concept or an action. For if it is an action, then fittingly the baptized brothers of the Word-made-flesh must live an active life of charity and not be totally bound to a conceptual religion. A conceptual religion without the consequent activity remains as dry as the pages on which such concepts are articulated.

Someone, however, may ask the basic question: Exactly where is the true Church to be found? In the visible structure or in the invisible spirit within each individual? The only correct answer is to say that the true Church is found in both, but—and this is important—the two aspects will never be perfectly reconciled in this life. The trick the Christian must perform is to exist in the visible, structured institution, while remaining ever sensitive to the freedom of the spirit within him.

This balancing act is hardly easy: to accept both, to reject neither. The easier way is to choose one or the other. Many of us, however, do not want to leave the visible Church, while at the same time we do wish to expend the effort to reconcile the visible structure with the invisible spirit of freedom. If we at least realize that a perfect reconciliation is impossible in this life, then we have learned what Jesus taught through his Incarnation: that man lives simultaneously in two distinct worlds without denying one or the other. The person who learns this lesson understands how to accept the tension without breaking apart. What I have suggested about the Church may be difficult to consider, but this it seems is where Jesus told us the Church lies in the first place.

CHRISTIAN HOPE,
LOVE,
AND CHARITY

Bow down, then, before the power of God now,
and he will raise you up on the appointed day;
unload all *your worries on to him*, since he is
looking after you. *Be calm but vigilant*, because your
enemy the devil is prowling round like a roaring lion,
looking for someone to eat [1 Peter 5:6-8].

MAN'S TRUST IN GOD

DR. REINHOLD NIEBUHR, the prominent Protestant
theologian has written: "Religious faith is basically
a trust that life, however difficult and strange, has
ultimate meaning." Life is a mystery, but God can
give life significance even if belief in God and trust
in God do not afford us complete comprehension of
life and its mystery. "Man's reach is always beyond
his grasp," says Dr. Niebuhr, echoing Robert Browning who wrote "Ah, but a man's reach should exceed his grasp,/Or what's a heaven for?" The poet
and the theologian, because both deal with the mys-

tery of life, often see the same thing and express the idea similarly. For if man's reach is always beyond his grasp, then man must trust that ultimately there is something more beyond this life for which he is reaching, but which in this life he is incapable of totally apprehending.

The need for trust today is obvious. Not a vague, misty, almost forlorn trust of which the poet Tennyson wrote:

> Behold, we know not anything;
> I can but trust that good shall fall
> At last—far off—at last, to all,
> And every winter change to spring.

There is solid reason for the Christian to trust, and that reason is the almighty God who has created our souls, who sustains our life, and who will judge us when this life for us has ended. Our motive for trusting is a God of love, a God who so loved the world that the Second Person of the Divine Trinity died to restore supernatural life to man.

Our need today for trust in someone permanent, unchanging, is obvious when we read of the human problems of our world. What is the average person to think about the war in Vietnam? We can read the writings of John C. Bennett of Union Theological Seminary, in which he calls for Christian realism to oppose the United States' involvement in that war. And we can read the words of Professor Paul Ramsey, professor of religion at Princeton University, who seriously questions what he calls the sweeping

126

moral judgments of Dr. Bennett and the Christian realists. At the moment we are confused. Experts disagree. Religious leaders and teachers disagree. Human judgments, in short, are quite fallible.

Our trust in God, then, is more and more necessary today because amid the rapid changes in our world and amid the tension largely created by the rapidity of mass communication media, we need something permanent.

There are two attitudes toward trust, neither of which seems wholly appropriate. One begins with the notion that this world is a vale of tears: accept it, don't fight it, do nothing about the evil in the world, but just trust in God. This attitude believes with Tennyson that somehow good will come from evil, and those who follow such an approach make a *felix culpa* out of everything from original sin to racial injustice. "Don't do; just accept" is their motto. It is a type of pietism.

The other attitude omits God from the scene. Since we cannot reason clearly to his existence, and since we cannot see him, forget about him. If God is not dead, he is at least a dead issue. There may or may not be an afterlife to worry about, so why bother about it. Some may even go so far as the poet Swinburne and say of man that "His life is a watch or a vision between a sleep and a sleep." Man came from nowhere, and ultimately he goes nowhere. We cannot see God's apparent interest and involvement in this world; therefore, live a totally human existence without reference to the divine.

The Christian attitude toward trust lies between these two extremes. The Christian should never become so rationalistic that he fails to trust in God in whom he believes. On the other hand, he never becomes so pietistic that he feels nothing can be done about the evils in the world. The Christian recognizes evil in the world, and if he is a committed Christian, he does what he can to relieve it. The Christian tries his best to see confusing situations as best he can in the light of Christian morality.

St. Peter reminds us in his letter that the devil goes about seeking whom he may devour. And either of the above-mentioned extreme positions is fair game for the beast. He can make the pietistic soul self-satisfied that God's in his heaven and all's right with my little world; as for anybody else, well each man must help himself. Or he may use the extremely rationalistic individual to keep people from trusting in God. The Christian attitude follows a middle course.

That is why I am telling you not to worry about your
life and what you are to eat, nor about your body and
how you are to clothe it. Surely life means more than food,
and the body more than clothing! [Matthew 6:25].

WHAT, ME WORRY?

EVERY AGE in history is described and classified
either by an attitude prevalent during that period or
by a reigning monarch or by a human situation existing at that time. Thus, we have the Age of the
Enlightenment, the Golden Age of Pericles, the Dark
Ages, the Victorian Period. Were we to attempt to
describe our own age, we might call it the anxious
age, the confused age, the age of the gadget or gimmicks, the age of the put-on and put-down. But fundamentally our age is an age of fear.

129

Since the conclusion of the Second World War, since Hiroshima, men have been afraid. The titles of books published since 1945 illustrate this point, books of all types and on all subjects: *The Conquest of Fear; Fear Not, Little Flock; A Fearful Joy; Fear Strikes Out; Childbirth Without Fear.* Newspapers, in reporting daily events, capitalize on this fear-filled temper of the times. Advertisers are extremely conscious of the motive of fear. There are a hundred little fears in the soul of men everywhere: fear of insecurity, fear of old age, fear of social unacceptability, fear of death.

The humor of today's world, our so-called sick comedy or black comedy, implies a sadism that is often a facade for personal fright of one's fellowman. Even that gross caricature of contemporary mores, *Mad Comics*, has put into the mouth of its hero Alfred E. Newman the ironic observation, "What, Me Worry?"

The brashness of the young, the sloth of workers, the do-as-little-as-possible theory that prevails today, are masks for a basic fear that if anyone in our democracy tries to surpass others he thereby endangers others. Let everyone, therefore, get away with as much as possible, with as little effort as possible, for as much money as possible. Let no one rock the boat in the name of trying harder or striving for excellence.

Those who question the standards of the past when excellence was worth achieving, those who want to rid the world of anything that our ancestors may have thought profitable, may protest and riot, but they offer little, if anything, of positive value to fill the void they create. The starry-eyed idealists on college campuses are doing their thing, but often enough they cannot tell you explicitly what that thing is or where it will lead them.

People are afraid to defend anything traditional, even when it might be right and proper. They are afraid of being labeled a square, afraid that they will be cropped from the big picture of life. Sam Levenson speaks humorously about the hierarchy of fear that exists today in the school system: "The teachers," he says, "are afraid of the principals; the principals are afraid of the superintendents; the superintendents are afraid of the parents; the parents are afraid of the kids; and the kids—they ain't afraid of anybody."

Our vision has been distorted because of our fears. We find ourselves afraid to follow a truly Christian pattern of life because vocal secularists have sold us on the idea that, since God is omnipresent in the world, the world by itself is sacred. This observation contains a truth, but the implication is that man therefore has no need of God if man contents himself only with service to men in this world alone.

We fear to get down to work. Students are afraid of academic effort because it means self-denial, and self-denial is the dirtiest word on campus. Parents fear to say an emphatic "No!" to children for fear that, if they do not acquiesce to the child's every whim, their children will develop frustrations. One of these days the affluent society will suffer, and then the choice will be between nihilistic agnosticism or saying an unequivocal "No!" to much of the nonsense in the world today. As a progressive educator remarked not long ago, "The progressive system in which a child is permitted to develop for himself has much merit, but there comes a time when a parent or a teacher has to say very simply, 'Sonny boy, you just have to do this, like it or not.'" There will come a time, if it has not already arrived, when men can no longer fearfully comply with the secular attitude, but will have to utter an emphatic denial to the romantic nihilists who are influencing thought on campuses.

The Christian may not have an answer to every contemporary problem. But the Christian does possess an antidote for fear. This antidote is the virtue of hope the Christian has through baptism. Christian hope is a confident expectation—relying not on ourselves but on the power and love of God's merciful omnipotence—that we shall surely succeed in the difficult task of one day achieving our destiny. This virtue, like any power given by God to man, must be developed by man in his day-to-day efforts to cope with the life situation.

The effect of supernatural hope is that it clears away man's anxiety and despondency; it precludes thoughts of discouragement; it allays our fears; it allows no room for anything approximating despair. This hope is a sharing in a joy which, although it begins in faith during this life, is fulfilled only in union with God after death. Hope enables man to share in God's own life here and now.

Yet today we are surrounded by the hucksters of the communications media, newspapers, magazines, and television suggesting to us new fears that are in reality trivial and ridiculous. A housewife fears her hands will be rough and red; man fears that the least headache or pain will cause social disaster; a family fears they haven't moved up to the right make and model of automobile. Advertising that surrounds us like the air we breathe develops man's tendencies to fear that his home will not equal his neighbor's in status, that his neighborhood is really not a proper address, that his children will not be enrolled in the proper schools. All these fears enter our lives, and to what good?

To calm these ever-present fearful naggings, man must constantly rely on the virtue of hope within him. Man must put his ultimate hope and trust not in this world, which passes away, but in the next life which remains forever.

The years since Hiroshima have witnessed a rise in secularism in all areas, religion not excluded. Lawmakers have handed down decisions that give the Christian pause. The famous prayer decision, though in itself not serious, has encouraged misguided groups to protest even the National Anthem because the name of God appears in one of the seldom-sung verses. There are movements to remove God's name from our coins, to rid our military forces of denominational chaplains, to dispense with a chaplain for our legislative bodies. We are indeed living amid the secular city that puts its hope not in God but solely in man.

An alumnus of a Catholic university whose son attended Harvard wrote not long ago that he was elated to find that his son, though he did not have the theological orientation of his father, had graduated with a strong secular spirit that prompted him to work mightily for social causes. We can admire the person who gives himself to the corporal works of mercy, indeed, but we may also question the sense of values of the individual who does the right thing for the wrong reason.

Perhaps in a pluralistic society there is little or nothing that an individual Christian, or even a group of Christians, can do to change the course of secularized events in this country. But each individual Christian can at least have the courage to lift up his eyes hopefully to look beyond this transient life to a more permanent existence with God. The Christian ought to avoid placing all his hopes in his home, in his nation, in his lawmakers, in his courts, in his family and friends. He ought rather to anticipate confidently and hopefully our dwelling place with God in heaven. Christian hope prompts man to look elsewhere than to this temporary city for his complete fulfillment.

The hopeful Christian need not let the world prey upon his fears. Fear degrades a man; it makes him bitter; it turns him into a beast. A piece of verse attributed to George Patton reveals what fear does to a person:

> I am that dreadful blighting thing
> Like ratholes to the flood,
> Like rust that gnaws the faultless blade,
> Like microbes to the blood.
>
> I spare no class or cult or creed,
> My course is endless through the year
> I bow all heads, and break all hearts.
> All owe me homage—I am Fear!

The words express in imagery what fear does to a man; quite simply, it makes him less a man. There is no doubt that it is easier to swim with the tide, to go along with the popular opinion polls, to declare that the Church is backward and out of step.

And yet we recall that the same was said about Jesus Christ. His Crucifixion was a stumbling block to some; to others it was simply folly. Certainly there are areas where the Church can and must adapt herself, and she will, but in her own time. She will adapt herself because in her wisdom she sees the rectitude of some adjustment.

Fear helps no one. Worry solves no problems. Worry leads to bitterness, to selfishness, to self-centeredness. The solid Christian hopes, because that hope reflects the omnipotence of God, the all-powerful God who is the source of truth. Jesus told us that we need not fret about clothes or basic necessities, because our heavenly Father knows that we need these things. Jesus reminds us of the need for the long-range view of hope. Hope is for the mature Christian. The immature Christian who lacks the patience necessary for hope is like the child to whom a wait of five minutes seems an eternity.

Young people grow impatient with older people. If such dissatisfaction is expressed respectfully, it is both refreshing and fruitful. The older person needs the vital outlook of youth. But youth needs the wisdom and experience of age. Just as the hand may not tell the eye that it has no need for it, so neither youth nor age may inform the other that there is no place for them on this earth.

Hope is a thing with feathers, for through hope we literally fly to God. Without hope, we have to rely solely on ourselves and on man. And only a fool would be willing to trust his total situation and ultimate significance to humanity, especially that humanity which has significance only because of the God in whom man must hope.

Set your hearts on his kingdom first, and on his righteousness, and all these other things will be given you as well [Matthew 6:33].

GOD IN THE

TECHNOLOGICAL AGE

ON TODAY's sophisticated college campus, perhaps, Jesus' injunction to seek first the kingdom of God falls upon uncomprehending ears. The words may even be so vague that they strike undergraduates nowadays as meaningless, especially since we are currently bombarded with observations that God is hidden or withdrawn from the world, or uninterested in man, or even dead.

Seeking God's kingdom and its justice (or seeking God and his approval) demands that we practice in this world the twin virtues that pertain to our social responsibilities: justice and charity. Thus, seeking God is hardly a blind leap into vague mistiness. The seeking of God's kingdom stands rooted fundamentally in our dedication to the immediate tasks at hand: raising a family, creating racial harmony, studying diligently, developing our intellects, assisting the poor, rehabilitating the social misfit, teaching young people, working for fairness in employment. All these activities presume charity and justice by which man seeks the kingdom of God. Amid these activities, then, the Christian's primary goal is always the seeking of God's kingdom.

These subordinate goals are very real: educating ourselves and others, creating a home and a family, working efficiently at our jobs, winning a golf game, enjoying a film. But transcending these goals is that primary purpose, seeking God through justice and charity. Other goals are good; they are, however, subordinate to the main goal.

In our world, obstacles arise as a very part of our culture with which the medieval world certainly did not have to contend. Today there are difficulties unknown to the rationalists of the eighteenth century and problems the romantics of the nineteenth century did not have to solve. Their problems—and they had them—are not ours. We must seek God amid a later twentieth-century situation, not that of the thirteenth, the eighteenth, the nineteenth, or even the earlier twentieth century.

This twentieth century of ours was summarized rather subtly, yet very perceptively, by a recent advertisement for North American Aviation. It read: "Supersonic supremacy is the absolute condition of America's future security. It is a day-to-day thing. It must grow with major advances." Consider the implication of that statement. It does not promise that a desperate day-to-day struggle for an ever-advancing atomic technology will confer upon us any new advantages; only that if we do not continually advance in physical power we will be worse off than before. This type of progress resembles the interlude in *Alice in Wonderland* where Alice had to run as fast as she could just to stay where she was. Instead of new gains, a supreme effort is required to prevent immeasurable losses. In other words, we are hardly in utopia; rather, we stand on the edge of destruction.

I do not know who first said "invention is the mother of necessity," but the observation seems at least as truthful as its more familiar antithesis. The Industrial Revolution, for instance, did not arise out of a necessity; industrialism became a necessity created by inventions. Neither the telephone, the automobile, the airplane, the supersonic bomber were necessities until their invention generated a social and industrial system that could no longer exist without them.

Perhaps these nonnecessary devices are advantageous as well as necessary. Most of us think so. The invention of the atom bomb was the first invention that caused a considerable number of thoughtful people to wonder if the necessity which its invention had created—the very necessity called to our attention by North American Aviation—was not too high a price to pay for any benefits we had gained. In a very real sense, the side effects are not outweighed by any likely benefits.

This phenomenon is significant for undergraduates who are seeking the kingdom of God. For they must do so amid a rapidly expanding technological world. And one of the major problems is to consider the possibility that before anything more is invented the question might well be asked: Of what further necessities, which may distract us from our primary need to seek the kingdom of God, will this invention be the mother?

Jesus assures us that if we seek first the kingdom of God our other needs will be supplied. I don't think Jesus had in mind all the somewhat artificial necessities our technological age has added to the list of requirements for gracious living. The needs Jesus speaks of were the basic needs of food and shelter. Color television, Mustangs, Princess telephones, air conditioning, and so forth—these are the needs that twentieth-century man has created from his inventions. They may be real needs for us, but the problem they raise is that in their midst it is more difficult to seek God's kingdom than it was in a less sophisticated period of Christianity.

Few of us are ready to retire to Brook Farm. Even if we all wanted to withdraw from our urban areas, there aren't enough Walden Ponds to accommodate each of us. Not too many wish to establish any pantisocracy on the banks of the Susquehanna. Yet the twentieth-century undergraduate can do at least this: he can stop and consider whether the necessities that a technological age has created for him are properly placed in perspective so that he can still seek first the kingdom of God.

He may not be able to withdraw from the world; perhaps he must live in a world of gadgets and gimmicks, of hard sells and soft sells. But the thoughtful Christian undergraduate can ask some hard questions: Is education merely a means to a worldly, materialistic goal, or is education to make a man more intelligent? Ought a college be selected because of what its gilded name can do for a man after graduation? Or is a college selected because of its commitment? Is marriage used as a source for human happiness, or is it merely a convenient social arrangement to be dissolved when the going becomes difficult? Are children being educated in justice and charity, or are children the projections of parents who expect their children to fulfill goals they themselves failed to achieve? Are these children being educated, or will they sustain the social prejudices learned from parents? Are the valid amusements of the twentieth century used to relax us so we will do a better job, or are amusements a series of escape mechanisms?

Truly, God is interested in this world, but God in his wisdom respects man's freedom. He lets us seek him, and we seek him among our fellowmen and amid the material conditions of our technological world. No longer may we rely on a piety that had relevance in an earlier age. Our seeking of God must be done in the practical day-to-day manner in which, for example, the white man and the Negro live in justice and charity side by side. Seeking God today eliminates any search for mere status. If we allow the effects of our technology to blind us either to God or to our fellowmen, we have failed to follow the command of Jesus to seek first the kingdom of God and his justice.

Then I saw *a new heaven and a new earth*; the first heaven
and the first earth had disappeared now, and there
was no longer any sea. . . . It will never be night again and
they will not need lamplight or sunlight,
because the Lord God will be shining on them. They will
reign for ever and ever [Revelation 21:1, 22:5].

TASTE WAS NO PROBLEM

AT PENTECOST

MY PRESENCE HERE is awkward. I am a teacher of
language and literature; most of you undergraduates are preparing for careers in science or commerce. I am a clergyman; you are laymen. I am
forty-five years old; you are in your twenties. I am
bald; many of you have a superfluity of that glorious commodity whose absence on my pate only
makes my heart grow fonder. I am a Jesuit; you are
normal. How, then, can our minds meet this morning? The gap is unbridgeable.

The poet W. H. Auden, in his poem "Prologue at Sixty" in *The Dyer's Hand*, speaks of that gap:

> Can Sixty make sense to Sixteen-Plus?
> What has my camp in common with theirs,
> With buttons and beards and Be-ins?
> Much, I hope.

And Auden assigns a reason for his confidence. Referring to Scripture he says: " In *Acts* it is written / Taste was no problem at Pentecost."

He was implying, I think, that the Holy Spirit supplies that unity needed by the pluralistic society to which we all pay lip service, but which we find desperately difficult to achieve. Gradually, and in some cases unwillingly, men and institutions are coming together and cooperating. White and black, Christian and Jew, young and old. Cooperative ventures follow upon pluralism. Pluralism demands mixtures, cultural and academic, racial and ethnic, religious and political. In this diversity lies strength; uniformity lacks vitality.

Pentecost was pluralistic; Pentecost was alive. Pentecost was the closest the early Christians came to the Pepsi generation. Because pluralism is dynamic, taste was no problem at Pentecost. Unity prevailed beneath the differences. Taste was a problem at Babel, that other scriptural phenomenon where men spoke in different tongues. Babel was a divisive encounter; Pentecost presented a unified front. The difference was the presence of the Spirit, the source of the peace of Jesus Christ.

144

In the Book of Revelation we read this morning, man beholds through metaphor that moment when neither church nor temple exists, when no institutions are necessary, for all will share fully the peace that Jesus bequeathed us, as John recorded in his Gospel. The passage from Auden's *The Dyer's Hand* reminds man, however, that he seeks this peace in a world today conditioned by physical force, a world basically inimical to the peace of Jesus. As Auden suggests, man strives for peace among an anonymous public, mute and inarticulate, hostile to that diversity which distinguishes pluralism inspired by the Spirit. The public levels all tastes; physical power, as possessed by industrial and military machines, moves insensitive to taste; but at Pentecost, because of the Spirit, taste was no problem. Differences were the norm. When the Spirit is present, man delights in personal differences. The Spirit cannot function in the narrow mind expecting the single option.

Man seeks peace amid absurd situations to which he accommodates himself only if he shares a sense of tragedy, or what Herbert Marcuse calls a "consciousness which facilitates acceptance of the misdeeds of society." Americans need a tragic sense if they will strive for genuine peace in their contemporary world.

Had Americans a tragic sense, our present anxiety would not startle us. After all, what is more Christian than frustration, than losing in order to gain, than dying in order to live, than giving in order to receive? Had we a tragic sense, as Michael Novak observed in the New York *Times*, we could perhaps admit military and political defeats, admit that the "heart of America" like the heart of any nation is not especially good and noble, but ambivalent; we could admit that our private and public lives are shot through with falsehood and betrayal and hypocrisy, revealed in the way men con their way through college, through their careers, and through life itself; we could admit our phoniness revealed in academic sloth, in cheating ourselves and others, in our failure to pray, in our denial of rights to others less fortunate, in our refusal to worship God.

This American pretense of innate goodness bitterly divides Christians in this country. Since each thinks himself good, he projects existing evils onto others. Middle Americans, as Novak points out, blame agitators and communists; radicals blame pigs and fascists; black militants blame honkies; women's lib blames male chauvinists; liberals blame reactionaries. We might go on to add that academics blame everybody; the laity blame the priests; priests blame the bishops; bishops blame the Jesuits; the Jesuits blame God. And we won't know for some time if the buck stopped there.

Peace doesn't prevail amid our pluralism because no one sees himself as guilty; we lack the tragic sense. As Lord David Cecil says, "We have lost the sense of sin, and that's why we haven't had genuine tragedy since the seventeenth century." A tragic sense of life, as writers from Ovid to Shakespeare to

Novak allow, urges that the moral plague resides not in others but in ourselves. The tragic sense, upon which interior peace is founded, does not find in American absurdity any reason for shock, or dismay, or escape from action. Shock, dismay, escape— these reactions are merely pathetic, but the tragic sense of life differs from pathos precisely because tragedy views persons as agents, not as victims. The moral gulf between Lear and Willy Lohman is vast.

Our American tragedy arises not because we are, as Dreiser maintained, pawns of determinism, but because we must act, as Novak urges, with a wisdom, a courage, an honesty, and a compassion that we simply do not as yet possess. Lacking these, we lack peace. We work toward the fulfillment of peace in Jesus Christ. Had our people and our leaders a tragic sense of life—instead of invoking that whimsical nonentity, the American dream—we would be less pretentious, and consequently would live more at peace with pluralism.

The Christian's struggle for peace involves an active assessment of the status quo in the light of Christian principles. Although Dylan Thomas writes about old age and death, his words may be accommodated to the young Christian's striving for peace in this anonymous world where men's souls are battered by the powers of technology:

Do not go gentle into that good night,
Old age should burn and rave at close of day;
Rage, rage against the dying of the light.

147

My brothers and sisters, do not go gently into this world made absurd by the raw greed of commerce and the simplistic brutality of the military. God's world is beautiful; man has made it absurd. If you will be agents for intelligent change in your chosen professions, you must burn and rage for the peace of Jesus Christ; rage against the putting out of the light of candor and peace. Fear no opposition. Disagreement has never proved the Christian wrong.

If I give away all that I possess,
piece by piece,
and if I even let them take my body to burn it,
but am without love,
it will do me no good whatever [1 Corinthians 13:3].

REQUIRED FOR GRADUATION:
INTELLIGENT LOVE

WHAT IS VERY NECESSARY for graduates of a Christian university today is an intelligent love, a love that embraces all people: friend and foe, those we like and those for whom we feel no instinctive attraction, those saints we know and those sinners. As Dostoevsky has said, "Love a man even in his sin, for that is the semblance of divine love and is the highest love on earth."

This intelligent love is a giving of self to others. Many people show their love for others through

149

contributions of money to charitable and welfare groups. Such charitable giving is necessary, of course, but unless the giving of money is accompanied by the giving of self such financial offerings may become only hollow and sterile tokens. A person gives himself in love through working for others and by being interested in others. Prior to such action, though, a person must be intellectually convinced of the need and the merit of love. That is why love must be intelligent, not merely a matter of the heartstrings, the movements of which may urge a loosening of the purse strings.

Undergraduates often are practical examples of this intelligent love. Having seen the need and the merit of such projects as tutoring the culturally deprived, or working in Appalachia, or serving the poor, they have given themselves wholeheartedly to this work. Employers who show genuine interest in their employees also illustrate that intelligent love that marks the Christian. A teacher's love is expressed by his personal concern for his students, and his greatest frustration ought to be the number of campus faces to which he cannot put a name. Intelligent love, based on a knowledge of the need for love, is expressed by an interest in others, by instructing others, by the effort to give oneself to the work and the projects to which he is committed as either student or employee.

Intelligent love is opposed to the stupid negative reaction one sometimes hears. A person's analysis of a situation or a person is summarized thus: "It's not that I like Richard Nixon; I just hate LBJ." "It's not that I like the Reds; it's that I hate the Dodgers." "It's not that I like Michigan State; it's that I hate Notre Dame." Such negative analyses—if they may even be called analyses—hinder the full expression of an intelligent love for which the Christian strives.

At an undergraduate dance once, a young girl asked me if I enjoyed the beat. I replied that I didn't quite understand that sort of music. "Oh," she replied, "you don't try to understand; you just enjoy." Unfortunately, undergraduates often transfer this same attitude to love. There is no attempt to understand; love is merely enjoyed. And it follows in such thinking that if sensible enjoyment is lacking, there is no love there. In giving of self, however, sensible enjoyment may not be present.

Yet love in some way must involve a giving of self. Giving money should be based upon some self-denial; giving time, upon self-sacrifice; thus, the effort involved in love demands that we overcome self-centered and slothful ways, whether this sloth is in our body, which doesn't want to work, or in our mind, which may be unwilling to rid itself of silly prejudice against someone because of the color of his skin or the clothes he wears or the way he combs his hair.

Western Union hasn't gotten the message. At the bottom of its forms for greeting-card messages are printed the words: "For only a few cents more, the word *love* may be added to any of the above texts." It might cost a few pennies more to add the word *love,* but adding the actuality of love to our lives costs a lot more in time, in thought, and in effort. For the man who is unwilling to think about love and its place in his life is unwilling to pay the price of love, a love that is intelligent because it demands first of a man that he comprehend the need for love.

If the university committed to Christianity has failed in at least one way, I would suggest that it is surely here: that academics have failed to make an intelligent love vital enough in the lives of those in the university community. Some graduates can today still leave the Christian university totally unconvinced that they are really prejudiced against certain people and certain things; some graduates still leave more impressed with their quality point average than with the wisdom to which they have been exposed; some graduates today still want to gain responsible positions in the commercial world with the least amount of effort. Such graduates have failed to see the unity of a Christian life that is centered on love and justice, on work and effort.

A recent Gallup poll on the topic of college graduates is interesting. Asked the greatest weakness of college graduates entering the business world today, businessmen responded in several ways. "Their attitude is too much of a 'give me' attitude. They don't want to contribute toward the growth and profits of the company," said one. Another said, "They tend to inflate the value of a college education. Engineers believe it below their status to start on a drafting board. Accountants don't want to start as bookkeepers. And they all seem bent on working a shorter day." And another, "You can't get them to budge off their chairs. They have no real desire to work at jobs except for those that please them. You can't motivate them." I would conclude that these graduates failed basically in a lack of love, a lack of intelligent love, which is shown by the effort of mind and body in our day-to-day tasks, in the giving of ourselves to our work and to others.

If this poll truly reflects the graduate of a Christian university, then someone—teachers, administrators, chaplains, students—has failed to show that one's love is proved by one's willingness to give himself totally to the task at hand, by one's sense of justice, by one's realization that he is part of a joint effort, the success of which depends on each one giving of himself. For this giving *is* love. The selfish traits that the commercial world thinks it observes in college graduates today are rooted in the graduates' moral code, whether they comprehend this fact or not. It is a moral code which is extremely self-centered. And if this self-centeredness continues as the basis of their code, they will never genuinely love anyone or anything except themselves. They will attain nothing but the opposite of true, intelligent love.

Questioned about the strengths of the university undergraduate, one businessman observed: "On the whole they are probably much better equipped than my contemporaries." There seems less problem, therefore, with college graduates in the matter of their knowledge of technique; their weakness, if I read the analysis correctly, lies rooted in their failure to give themselves. One may be very gifted, one may be well trained, but if one has never learned to give himself—in work, in study, in prayer, in life— then one has failed in the basic requirement of love.

Love is the one thing that cannot hurt your
neighbour; that is why it is the answer to every one
of the commandments [Romans 13:10].

LOVE AND SELF-DECEPTION

THAT OLD ADAGE about the devil's ability to quote
Scripture for his own purposes need not necessarily
apply whenever anyone uses a passage from the
Bible to support a particular thesis. Some persons
tend, however, to select certain maxims from Scripture while neglecting, perhaps unconsciously, the
total contextual situation. Often a person will cite
chapter thirteen from Paul's letter to the people of
Rome to support a general notion about love:
"Love," they argue from Paul, "is the complete ful-

fillment of the law." Therefore, love, not obedience, fulfills the law; and love transcends the law. So if I act out of love, that action must be good.

One problem that immediately arises, however, concerns the proper analysis of love, for Paul nowhere says that man ought to say to himself, "I love, I love," and then do whatever he pleases. Paul does remark that man must "live the truth in love." This living the truth in love is quite different from the philosophy that the end justifies any means whatsoever, which is the root of the notion that one may adopt any moral posture as long as one's motive is love.

More important still, though, is the context of Paul's letter to the Romans. For Paul's treatment of love can only be understood against the background of the whole chapter:

> Let everyone submit himself to the ruling authorities, for there exists no authority not ordained by God. And that which exists has been constituted by God. Therefore he who opposes such authority resists the ordinance of God, and they that resist bring condemnation on themselves (Romans 13:1-2).

In the light of the above verses, how should we read Paul's observation that "he who loves his neighbor has fulfilled the law"? Paul's summary of God's commandments as contained in the imperative "Love your neighbor as yourself" serves to illustrate that though love may pervade all commands to do good

156

and avoid evil, love does not substitute for obedience to these commands.

Obviously, by introducing these verses into a discussion of love, one runs the risk of alienating the ACLU, *Commonweal*, the *National Catholic Reporter*, and nearly every person under the age of twenty-one. Nevertheless, the risk must be taken because in the matter of love the danger of self-deception is very real.

Self-deception in moral matters—and love and authority concern the moral lives of all of us—is frequent enough that one ought instinctively to fear any judgment made on a single scriptural text drawn out of context. Self-deception occurs often enough in nonmoral matters. Even TV commentators have learned to be careful about stating apodictically that there is only one way to function. It is not always necessary to punt on fourth down; it depends on circumstances. We run a daily risk of deceiving ourselves, almost unwittingly, if we are not careful to exercise a clear, sober judgment on the complete situation.

There is a story I've heard of a young man who went into a Cape Cod restaurant. When the headwaiter informed him there would be a one-hour wait for a table, he replied: "That's all right. My wife and I will wait in the bar." Into the bar they went and ordered a drink. As the bartender served them their drinks, though, the young man remarked in a tone audible enough for most of the others at the bar to hear, "Say, did you hear that the Coast

Guard just captured the largest whale ever, only two miles up the coast?" The bartender merely nodded, but the word spread along the bar and into the adjoining dining room. People suddenly began to leave and after about five minutes the headwaiter approached the couple to say, "Sir, we have a table for you." "Oh good," said the wife, "aren't you coming, dear?" "No, honey," the husband answered, "let's go see that whale." Self-deception may not always be so obvious, but to deny its effects on us is to be more than a little naïve.

The remedy for self-deception in the matter of love is found in following a norm. For the Christian, the ultimate norm is God. This was Paul's ultimate norm. He saw love within the framework of authority. He says clearly that the source of all authority is the Creator, God, the judge of man. Paul assumes as his starting point the idea of the people of God, the family that God has created through grace, whereby man becomes a child of the Father, a brother of Jesus Christ, and a dwelling for the Holy Spirit. In the context of this image of the family, man is motivated by love to obey—but he does not thereby deny the role of authority or law.

Should a man decide to live a life of love according to his own personal definition and apart from any norm, he deceives himself. In fact, he will destroy himself, for the law is there to enable man to love. Whether an individual law passed by some civil power is morally sound may be a moot point; and a man may resist positive injunction in the name of a higher law. The main point, however, is clear: law and love are not mutually exclusive; they are not at war with each other. You simply don't have one without the other.

Paul's choice of discussing both law and love in the same passage surely indicates that both are necessary for the Christian. Paul, despite what some may read into his letters, is not denying the law; his position is one of emphasis. Love transcends the law, but the law is to be obeyed. Law without love is sterile; love without law leads to anarchy. Love tends to be blind; we must try to see and to comprehend clearly. Unless we keep a clear head, unless judgments are sober, unless the Christian sees all sides of the scriptural message of Paul, he tends to deceive himself, and that way lies moral madness.

He went up and bandaged his wounds, pouring
oil and wine on them. He then lifted him on to his own mount,
carried him to the inn and looked after him [Luke 10:34].

CHRISTIAN SELF-DENIAL
AND CHARITY

A CHARGE sometimes leveled at Christianity is that
its attitude toward life is totally negative. For some
people, Christianity is a summary of prohibitions, a
list of actions not to be done, a litany of "No, No."
Admittedly, there are negative aspects to the Christian code, but Christianity is thereby neither moral
nor unique. A rather solid religious code is the Ten
Commandments, the fundamental moral law of
western man. That decalogue, you will recall, contains a series of prohibitions.

Whether the approach to morality through prohibition is psychologically more sound than an approach with fewer negative maxims is a moot point. Is it for example more effective to say, "Be honest and just in all dealings with others," or to say, "You shall not steal"? A negative imperative seemingly possesses a directness and a concreteness that a positive command may lack. And Jesus surely appears somewhat negative in the directive he offered people: "Unless you deny yourselves, unless you change your way of thinking, you will perish" (Luke 13:3). Hardly a veiled threat.

Yet Christianity is not solely negative, and the charge that it *is* merely underlines the fundamental error of those with a truncated view of Christianity. Behind any prohibition in the Christian code lies a positive purpose. Christianity demands self-denial, not for itself, but to enable a man to place charity, the love of God and the love of neighbor, above the love of self. Unless man willingly denies himself, he will never love anybody or anything except himself.

Husbands and wives fully realize that a life of self-denial on the part of both of them necessarily underlies a life of love. In the business world, only the man who denies himself succeeds. In the academic community, only the student who denies himself merits top grades. The businessman must sacrifice his own time to assure himself of advancement. The student must deny himself some partying if he will develop himself intellectually. The athlete, too, must deny himself if he wishes to be part of a successful team. The hot-dog athlete or the prima donna mars the team effort, because he is less interested in success than in his own career and his own self-satisfaction.

Self-denial, while negative, is directed always toward a positive goal, and it is in this light that Christian self-denial must be understood. The person who caricatures Christianity as a negative way of life, therefore, has failed to apprehend the total Christian plan. He has not realized that self-denial is required to respond fully to love, the great command of Jesus Christ.

The cry of self-fulfillment is heard often these days, particularly from the young. Generally speaking, though, their notion of self-fulfillment differs hardly at all from what the world would judge to be self-satisfaction. Self-fulfillment, for many young people, means they can do whatever satisfies them here and now, without any consideration of law, or the rights of others, or a code of moral behavior. The young person who says he is "fulfilling himself" is just as likely to declare that he is not one of those negative Christians, but a positive humanist. Penance, self-denial, mortification, self-sacrifice are all terms with distasteful overtones to him. Instinctively withdrawing from these words, he cries for the world to hear, "Accentuate the positive; eliminate the negative."

Those who consider self-fulfillment in these dimensions, however, should never logically disapprove of the actions of a Hitler or a Stalin. For them the words of Polonius, that most hollow of Shakespeare's characters, serve as a suitable guideline for life: "This, above all, to thine ownself be true, and it must follow as the night the day, thou canst not then be false to any man." Being true to oneself, though, however self-oriented it was to the mind of Polonius, does not suggest such a direction in the Christian dispensation. Browning's Duke of Ferrara was still a murderer for all his suaveness and urbanity. In his self-centered way, he was true to himself. Lear felt he was being true to himself and only later did he realize that throughout his life he had been morally blind. He had been concerned largely with personal self-satisfaction, which he mistakenly identified with self-fulfillment.

The positive must be accentuated perhaps, but this positive implies a negative. Love demands self-denial, and those who twist self-denial into a mere negative norm and seek only self-satisfaction turn self-fulfillment into self-love.

St. Luke recounts the story of the man from Samaria, that Good Samaritan who denied himself to show his love, his charity, for another. He literally fulfilled himself by denying himself. His time, his effort, his money, his very compassion all demanded a self-denial and all manifested a man genuinely true to himself. His self-denial was a necessary condition for his act of love.

Self-denial is the prelude to genuine love. Jesus stressed this fact in his teaching; Christianity proposes this doctrine; the Church in her teaching supports this idea. Positive love is the basis of Christian living, but to be effective this love demands self-denial. Far from being a negative manner of living because of its emphasis on self-denial, then, Christianity is obviously most positive if we look to the reason behind our denial of self: the freeing of self for love of God and love of neighbor, the great commands of Jesus.

My prayer is that your love for each other may
increase more and more and never stop improving your
knowledge and deepening your perception so that you can
always recognise what is best. This will help you to
become pure and blameless, and prepare you for the
Day of Christ [Philippians 1:9-10].

CHARITY AND

FUNCTIONAL LIVING

IN HIS LETTERS, St. Paul never tires of the theme of
love. And rightly so, since charity is the paramount
virtue for the Christian. Without charity, Christians
are simply shells, hollow persons, lacking the very
substance of a rich spiritual life. And charity is to
be directed toward both God and our fellowmen.
Love of God and love of neighbor, as Jesus of Nazareth makes quite clear, are one and the same. Paul
prays that this charity grow richer and richer. Paul
says that he trusts this love will be accompanied by

165

knowledge and insight, so that through love a man will learn to appreciate true values. Charity, then, is eminently practical; charity adds a necessary dimension to man's life.

Love may all too easily remain a happy abstraction, however, for the halfhearted Christian who is lazy, who merely wears the name of Christian. The Christian hears the moving story of the Good Samaritan and instinctively identifies with him. The difficulty is that the average Christian could just as easily be a modern counterpart of the two who passed by, the two who couldn't have cared less, who didn't give a tinker's curse about the wounded man at the side of the road.

Charity is the Christian's heritage. The early Christians, we are told, were distinguishable from other citizens by their charity, by their love within the group. But today there is a tendency merely to erect a facade of charity. The Christian who does little more than project an image, though, is either dishonest or deceived. Perhaps both. Think of the difference between character and reputation: A man's reputation is what others think of him; his character is what he really is. If a man expends vast amounts of energy to enhance his reputation without attending to his character, he deceives himself in a most pitiable manner. Similarly, Christians who concentrate on an image of charity at the expense of the reality are sham Christians.

The demands of charity are sometimes quite difficult to fulfill, yet that difficulty is scarcely sufficient reason for neglecting the love of others. And if the Christian remains self-centered in his social dealings, or in his worship of God, or in his attitude toward contemporary problems, he will hardly work at making himself God-centered as his vocation as a Christian demands. He will not arrive through charity at a sense of true values.

A Christian's lack of a sense of true values is never more obvious than in the case of prejudice. Such prejudice may be either subtle or obvious. "I am not prejudiced against the black man," says the nominal Christian, "I just don't want him living next door to me." Still another nominal Christian blatantly declares, "I don't like the blacks, and that's that. I don't want them anywhere around." Both men are prejudiced, though one man's prejudice is perhaps somewhat less subtly expressed than the other. Neither has a Christian attitude. And yet both may very well call themselves vital members of a Christian church.

Now prejudice is never reasonable. It is like the man who asked his wealthy friend for a loan of a hundred dollars. "Can't do it," said the wealthy friend, "my mother-in-law is visiting us right now." The man was puzzled at this response. "But what has that got to do with lending me a hundred dollars?" "Nothing at all," said the wealthy friend, "but when you don't want to do something, one excuse is as good as another."

Not long ago I read that white people did not want to live near black people because Negroes are shiftless, lazy, irresponsible, criminal, simply unintelligent, and unwilling to assist one another. Those same people also did not like Jews, because Jews are too ambitious, too clannish, too clever, too studious on how to get ahead, too willing to assist one another, and they also run many flourishing business enterprises.

What is significant about these absurd generalizations is that if you don't like somebody or something for some silly reason, then one excuse is as good as another; the facts really do not matter. And prejudice is by definition a prejudgment, not based on facts. It is diametrically opposed to a charity that leads to an appreciation of true values. In a prejudiced person there is hardly that full knowledge which, Paul says, accompanies love. That human anomaly, the prejudiced Christian, is simply unable to grow in charity. He hardly perceives, much less practices, a true sense of values. He is really a walking lie.

The Christian who fully assists at Mass and generously participates in community liturgy becomes aware of the social dimension of life. Worshiping together does more than merely symbolize the wider application of charity through social justice. The sacrifice of the Mass is a public official act of worship whereby a group of Christians participate together in the acknowledgment of God. The Mass is neither a priest's private prayer nor that one occasion each week when an individual reads his own devotional prayers. The Mass is public worship; it is group worship; it is official worship.

For that reason, moreover, the Mass demands that all who share in its effects participate through group worship. Group worship is achieved overtly through vocal response, community prayer, and community song. Group worship at Mass symbolizes the union among Christians as members of Christ's body, the Church. Furthermore, it represents brotherhood, and when Christians approach the communion table together, they exemplify their love in Christ for one another.

Yet even in the matter of worship, prejudice enters. How often an undergraduate says that he likes to "say his own prayers" during Mass, that he wants to go directly to God through private prayer even during a public liturgical action. What he is actually saying is that he doesn't want to join the group. There is nothing wrong with private prayers, but they have their place. The public worship of God at Mass, however, hardly seems the appropriate place.

Paul speaks of the need for Christians to develop that keen practical insight that accompanies charity. Elsewhere he states that personal salvation and sanctification for the Christian result from participation with the community. Paul's prayer applies quite well to our social prejudices: our prejudice toward group worship as well as our prejudice toward total acceptance of all our brethren. Insight, knowledge, and, above all, charity are necessary if the Christian is to avoid living a lie, living a life according to his own personal prejudices.

This has taught us love—that he gave up his life for us; and
we, too, ought to give up our lives for our brothers.
If a man who was rich enough in this world's goods saw
that one of his brothers was in need, but closed his
heart to him, how could the love of God be living in him?
My children, our love is not to be just words or mere talk,
but something real and active [1 John 3:16-18].

LOVE AND SELF-INTEREST

ST. JOHN'S first epistle summarizes Jesus' teaching
as John himself considered it. Among the theological
points John discusses are the obligations of Christians not merely to avoid sin, but to act positively
by showing their love for their neighbor. This love
must so fill the Christian's soul that it is not restricted to lip service—which all Christians pay to
charity—but is proved by action.

As we read St. John's letter, we observe a relatively simple style in sentence structure, but not al-

170

ways a strict coherence among sentences. Yet John's coherence is found not in his syntax, but in his tone, in the very manner whereby he relates his observations on man in a few telling points. And the pivotal issue of the third chapter is the need for a vital human love proved by deeds.

To love his neighbor actively requires that a Christian force himself out of his own petty attitudes, lift himself from the pit of self-centeredness. Contemporary advertising illustrates this point. John Leo recently singled out in his column in *Commonweal* a catalog from a New York merchandiser that listed the following items indicating how far advanced our society is: an electric hairbrush, a battery-operated pepper mill, a lemon-twist knife, a goose-quill toothpick, an instant glass froster, an egg scissors for cutting the tops off soft-boiled eggs, an electric sweater dryer, an electric "sleep sound" that lulls one to sleep scientifically with a blend of appropriate rhythmic tones designed to counteract the nighttime clamor from cars, airplanes, and, presumably, from the noise of electric hairbrushes, pepper mills, and sweater dryers. We may smile at the thought of purchasing any of these gadgets, but the merchandiser knew very well that he could successfully market these items because each of them catered to some aspect of human self-interest, to man's desire to make the littlest annoyance in his life even less annoying if possible.

Behind this drive in man to have things as perfect as possible lies that basic self-centeredness which proves an obstacle to active charity toward the neighbor. Christianity demands, therefore, that man work against this selfishness and work toward loving his fellowman. In a somewhat offhand manner St. John tells us that since Jesus laid down his life for men, the Christian must be willing to do likewise for his fellowman. Our Christian lives are not fully Christian unless and until they are lived rather for others than for ourselves.

One obvious manifestation of un-Christian self-centeredness is a tendency for a man to withdraw into his own world where he wishes not to be bothered by others. His own problems, he says, are sufficient and the last thing he needs is to assume the problems of others. Such an attitude will lead an individual into a progressively more narrow world. The university professor, for instance, may become so involved in his private research that he has no time for students. A businessman may be so concerned about his business affairs that he takes no time to consider his workers and their families. Neighbors may be so concerned about their own neighborhood that, in their fears, they will keep it white at all costs.

To accommodate such parochial self-interest to the description of true Christianity recorded by St. John seems impossible. Yet the attempt is made regularly, the excuses offered. Teachers say they love the students, but they do not care to meet them informally. An employer claims to be interested in workers' output, but not in their personal problems.

172

Neighbors claim to have no prejudice against the Negro; they just don't want blacks living next door.

Any area that requires Christians to be active in their charity toward others will always present difficulties. These problems with the practice of Christianity in the concrete arise, however, simply because baptism does not remove the fundamental self-centeredness in Christians. The Christian who fails to take the initiative in working for others, in being interested in others, the Christian who even recoils from thinking about his brother's problems is not really a Christian at all in anything but name.

Christians must learn to rise above their tiny world of self-interest. Possibly because of the influence of the evangelicals of the middle class in the nineteenth century, we have come as a nation to believe that our own material prosperity indicates God's blessing, that poverty is a sign of God's displeasure. Perhaps we may even be naïve enough and brutal enough and uncharitable enough to think that all people who are poor are poor precisely because they are too lazy to work. We want them to do what supposedly we have done: pull themselves up by their own bootstraps.

St. John asks quite bluntly how the love of God lives in that man who, having the goods of this world and seeing his brother in need, closes his heart to him. The Christian must be willing to help. Wealthier parishes should share their goods with poorer parishes. Talented undergraduates should assist in those tutoring programs that exist in every large city. But to do this, Christians must work against a self-centeredness.

To hear the Scripture on Sunday morning is easy; to read the Scripture is relatively simple. But unless these words penetrate the hearts of Christians, the hearing and the reading of Scripture remain sterile experiences. Christianity is not to be analyzed or contemplated; it must be lived. In that famous parable from Luke's Gospel, a number of excuses are offered for failures to attend a banquet to which many had been invited. How true to life! How easy it is for Christians to find excuses for not actively loving their neighbors! Yet St. John tells us that love of neighbor is the very hallmark of the Christian.

Genuine love of God is proved by active love of neighbor. For Christians to love their neighbors in contemporary circumstances, it may be necessary to rethink some attitudes, to reevaluate some current thinking. Yet today's situation is the only one we shall ever have. It is the situation that faces us now as Christians, as those who are expected to love the neighbor, as Christ loved us. If a Christian is called to heroism, we know, he must lay down his life for his neighbor, as Jesus did for all of us. But before we nominal Christians start thinking about dying for our neighbor, we would do well to think about living for him.

FOR CHRISTIANS:

MORALITY AND

A LIFE OF PRAYER

I have fought the good fight to the end;
I have run the race to the finish;
I have kept the faith [2 Timothy 4:7].

CONFUSION IS
OUR MIDDLE NAME

WHENEVER a Christian undergraduate approaches me with the observation, "I'm confused about this . . . ," I am inclined to reply, "Welcome to the human race." If there is a common denominator among many Christian undergraduates today, it is neither long hair nor sideburns, neither a mode of dress nor a manner of speech; it is confusion. And with good reason: older Christians are confused.

If religion and morality appear more and more relative to the Christian undergraduate, it may well be because theologians, preachers, teachers, and moralists appear unwilling these days to defend any absolute position with much vigor. I am not referring here to the intransigent reactionaries who have hardly done enough thinking to be confused, nor to the free-swinging religious anarchists who are largely liberal as long as their own intellectual route is followed. I am thinking here of the large body of intelligent moderates among Christians.

The average Christian today, and hence the average Christian undergraduate, is hung up, is tense, is in a bind in many religious and moral areas. Teachers, students, priests, laymen, now that the apodictic approach has been largely abandoned, are confused. It's been a topsy-turvy world ever since the Dodgers left Brooklyn and the Yankees ceased to dominate the American League. No wonder people have decided that God is dead.

Any thinking Christian could recite his own litany of opposed religious attitudes on the same question. The pages of the *National Catholic Reporter* render, sometimes sensationally, the varieties of opinions prevailing in the minds of different Christians on vital subjects.

As regards celibacy, for instance, some maintain that married priests would be living in baptized concubinage, while others declare that only a non-celibate life will assist the priest in his total fulfillment as a human person.

Some Christians accept the pill as a normal procedure; others believe it is a direct contravention of

God's law. The Christian can usually find the right confessor to espouse his particular views; word does manage to get around.

When the Friday abstinence became optional, some Catholics breathed a sigh of relief and muttered, "Well, it's about time." Others felt that for a Catholic to eat meat on Friday indicated that the end of the world was fast approaching.

Liturgical celebrations, often following forms that appeal only to the local pastor, offer more confusion. In some parishes a priest still reads the Liturgy of the Word in Latin with his back to the people. Or he may offer Mass at many a high school to the accompaniment of guitars, drums, and saxophones.

Vietnam is a crucial issue. There are the peaceable words of Pope Paul VI and the patriotic exhortations of the late Cardinal Spellman. And on many a Christian campus one finds pacifists and conscientious objectors rubbing shoulders with ROTC men.

Charles Davis leaves the priesthood and marries. "See," say some, "how the Church ruins a good man." "Charles Davis is a disloyal priest," is uttered in reply. Sister Jacqueline leaves her religious community and changes the character of her college from a Christian school to a secular institution. How does the Christian world react? "More power to her!" "She just faked out her entire congregation."

Civil rights has divided Christians because of confused thinking. Priests lead protest marches in support of open housing; pastors preach that their parishes are not ready for integration.

Those of us engaged in higher education hear the comment that Catholic colleges must be more academically selective, and from the same people we hear that Catholic colleges are not doing enough for the culturally deprived. For some, Catholic schools are too snobbish; for others, Catholic schools today lack prestige.

Not long ago the seminarians in a large archdiocesan institution demanded, and were granted, a greater voice in the conduct of seminary affairs. Hardly a month later, after they had active voice in most proceedings, they were protesting the lack of leadership from the seminary administration.

Students in colleges all want more responsibility, yet rather than be given a bibliography for a theology course, they prefer the teacher to stick to a single text that students can memorize and give back on true-false examinations.

Clearly, as this litany of opposites indicates, there is confusion among Christians. Each of us could catalog his own list of opposites regarding problems in Christianity today that tend to confuse us. And each of us has his own solutions, too, which often do little to dispel confusion.

Ten years ago I probably would have taken a strong, definite stand on any one side of these issues. Today I frankly don't know. Perhaps this is the coward's approach; perhaps I have abandoned all principles; maybe I'm just playing it cool and not getting bothered. I like to think, however, that I am following the injunction "in essentials unity, in nonessentials liberty, in all things charity," which seems a pretty good norm for confused moments.

A priest recently remarked, "I don't know what the Church stands for any longer. I could recommend the Marine Corps to a young man because I know what the Marines stand for, but I doubt if I could recommend the Church." Perhaps this view, somewhat overstated, is the attitude of many a Christian. Nevertheless, the Church still stands for the Apostles' Creed; the Church is still a teacher. The difference today lies less in what the Church represents than in what individual Christians are shouting at the top of their lungs that they believe— or at least wish to believe.

The Church, I think, is large enough for all the opposed opinions as long as they do not contradict explicit teaching of the Church, because the Church is Christ's witness in history. The Church will withstand all the turmoil that now rises within her and among her members, because Christ is with the Church until the end of time. The Church is strong enough to embrace all parties even when they differ among themselves. The Church can handle both Democrats and Republicans.

Amid all the confusion today, though, there is a great need for intellectual calmness. The Church is passing through an exciting, but nonetheless a turbulent, period. Mutiny is threatening Peter's bark from all sides: from those Catholic intellectuals and academics for whom freedom is an end not a means; from those parents who want to control family size in any way whatsoever; from priests who feel celibacy to be a major obstacle to their personal fulfillment; from nuns who feel constrained by rules and customs established in the past that have only the accidental sanction of domestic tradition; from young people who prefer the action at the local drive-in to Christian commitment; from undergraduates who, despite their eagerness, are not sufficiently mature to appreciate the role of mystery in both God and man (in both literature and theology).

One solution that some have found satisfying is to leave the Church entirely. God wills the eternal happiness of all men; he has established his Church as the means to attain this ultimate goal. But if an individual wishes to reject a Church that teaches and governs, then perhaps he ought to have the guts and the intellectual conviction to act on his conviction. It seems stupid to remain half in, half out. Yet even these people perhaps are confused, without any real intellectual conviction regarding the Church's teachings and laws; they just rely on their personal stirrings felt along the heart. In other words, they want the Church on their own terms.

Another solution to today's turmoil and tension is to remain in the Church and to continue to try one's best to live according to her teachings amid all the furor, amid all the defections, amid all the confusion. To go totally secular, as some have done, seems suspect, for it indicates a lack of genuine commitment to God. A new ecclesiastical structure may be forthcoming, but all in due time. We need patience.

If God's existence is questioned by theologians, this need not lead the Christian undergraduate to assume immediately that God is really dead. God has outlasted many a theologian. The Church's way of life is undergoing reorganization, but all tradition has not been abandoned. Our age may some day prove to have been the best of times or the worst of times; what seems apparent is that we are simultaneously experiencing a spring of hope and a winter of despair. The Christian undergraduate must keep a sane head on his shoulders through the variety of seasonal changes.

As we reflect on all this contemporary confusion, Paul's letter to Timothy comes to mind. It is consoling to think over again his words about that faithful soul who, once life is concluded for him, will receive the merited crown. If the Christian has been faithful to God through fidelity to his teaching Church, if the priest has preached the Word, if the layman has heard the Word, if we have all borne with difficulties and suffered frustrations, if we have, finally, fought the good fight and run the good race and have kept faith, reward eventually awaits us. When confused, it's a good idea to think about eternal life.

If you live according to your lower nature
you will die;
but if by the spirit you put to death
the deeds prompted by your lower nature,
you will live [Romans 8:13].

THE SPIRIT OF GOD

AND THE GOOD LIFE

IN THE EIGHTH CHAPTER of his letter to the people
of Rome, after he has spoken about the Spirit of God
working jointly with our own soul, after he has declared that grace works within us, St. Paul reminds
us Christians of the need to live a genuinely spiritual
life, of the necessity to avoid leading the unspiritual
life that in reality is spiritual death. "If you live according to your lower nature," says Paul, "you will
die; but if by the spirit you put to death the deeds
prompted by your lower nature, you will live."

184

Today, when man appears guided largely by his external senses, he tends to accept only what he can readily observe with his eyes or hear with his ears or touch with his hands. To declare that the Spirit of God inspires man and influences him sounds as naïve as the notion that the Mets will win the pennant in October because they lead the National League in May. When Christians become concerned, as they are today, with a visibly active Christianity asserting itself in social work, in welfare programs, in love-ins, words about the intangible Spirit of God strike one as passé. Talking about the Spirit of God is like discussing the great pumpkin. Let's face it! Who today has ever seen or touched or heard this Spirit of God?

Scriptural evidence for the Spirit of God, of course, is impressive. Paul emphasizes this Spirit in the eighth chapter of his letter to the people of Rome. The Christian must choose either to accept the Spirit of God, which enters his soul at baptism and develops within him at every advance in grace, or to reject the Spirit of God as a pious fable or a lovely metaphor that is groundless and has no practical bearing on man's life.

This Spirit of God, as he appears in Scripture, works concurrently with our human freedom. This Spirit moves, prompts, suggests, urges, assists, and exhorts. Never, however, does the Spirit coerce. Man maintains his freedom, and consequently man may reject the promptings of the Spirit of God in his free choices.

If man rejects the Spirit of God, Paul declares, man has decided to live by the flesh. Unspiritual choices of the flesh occur when the Christian either does not advert to the Spirit of God or fails to conform his soul to the Spirit of God. The Christian may violate the first commandment by his unspiritual choices, for he thereby substitutes alien gods for the one true Spirit of God. For instance, he substitutes sex for love; he considers financial security the primary reason for his education; he places worldly prestige above moral rectitude. The unspiritual undergraduate selects a school for its prestige image without even considering that school's educational philosophy or basic commitment. The unspiritual parent, in a misguided burst of democracy, allows his children equal voice with himself in domestic decisions.

In the Gospel Jesus praises the shrewdness of the unjust steward in material matters. Jesus regrets that the spiritual person, the child of light, the Christian, fails to act as intelligently in spiritual matters. Prior to every important decision, does the spiritual Christian say, "What does God expect me to do?" or "What will be in the best spiritual interests of my family?" Is his choice based fundamentally on what is spiritually most profitable?

Whether he should play tennis or sit glued to the television is not necessarily a major decision for the Christian. But decisions concerning charity toward the neighbor, social justice for all residents of a city, a full day's work in return for wages, the honest manufacturing of a product, the choice of education for his children—areas where charity and justice must prevail—in all these decisions the spiritual man should be led by the Spirit of God, not by the flesh.

The Spirit of God is active in our concrete decisions, which may be made for either spiritual motives or for unspiritual motives. The shrewd, unjust steward was a man of the flesh, an unspiritual man, but he acted in accordance with his principles. The Christian today, if he will avoid being swept along in the current of agnostic secularism, must act in accord with the Spirit of God. And the Christian who acts in accord with the Spirit of God does not merely pay lip service to a hierarchy of values; this hierarchy of values influences his daily choices. Obedience is not something we talk about; it is an action which children owe parents, which men owe authority.

Sacrifice to God did not end with Calvary; it is continued in history in the sacrifice of the Mass and in the personal sacrifices each of us is called upon to make in his daily life. Certainly we live in a material world, but we must so live in the Spirit that the demands of this material world never usurp the primary position occupied by God. If man is led by the Spirit, God will not be dislodged by his position.

I want to remind you, brothers,
how our fathers were all guided by a cloud above them
and how they all passed through the sea. . . .
all ate the same spiritual food
and all drank the same spiritual drink, . . .
In spite of this, most of them failed to please God
and their corpses littered the desert [1 Corinthians 10:1-5].

MAN'S MORAL ATTITUDE

MAN PROGRESSES through history, so we are told.
Both a material evolution and a spiritual evolution
occur. Darwin declared that man develops toward
the perfect specimen; Teilhard de Chardin wrote
about man's advances spiritually toward point
omega. Because of this evolution, though, man
tends to think that twentieth-century man differs
vastly from the people of Corinth to whom Paul
wrote in warning, "Therefore, whoever believes he
is standing firm, should beware lest he fall" (1 Corinthians 10:12).

188

Perhaps because we feel that we differ from them, we decide that Paul's words have little or no significance for us today. We are more sophisticated than the ancient Israelites, whose sins Paul recounts. We are more knowledgeable than the Romans, whom Paul warned against pagan stupidity. We are not nearly as carnal as those beastly Corinthians. Paul warns the people of Corinth against becoming idolaters, like some of the ancient Israelites who danced before the golden calf. Paul reminds the Corinthians that they are not to commit fornication, nor to try the Lord's forbearance, nor to murmur against God. As Paul says about these occurrences, "All these things happened to them to serve as examples" (1 Corinthians 10:11).

They are no less examples for us today than for the Corinthians. Indeed, as a man reflects upon Paul's words he realizes that even today we have idolaters, not of a golden calf but of the golden nugget. He recognizes that fornication and adultery are still committed, only now it is called self-fulfillment by some. He understands that God may not be tempted as much by sins of presumption as by actual denial. Quite simply, then, he realizes that what Paul wrote to the people of Corinth could also be written to twentieth-century Americans.

Times do change—perhaps for the better, perhaps for the worse. The judgment of our age's superiority over another age depends on your viewpoint of course. In the last century a person could be arrested for fighting or for adultery. Now we can watch either any night of the week on television. Whether this cultural development redounds to our credit or to our shame depends on our basic moral attitude.

It is this moral attitude, too, that conditions a man's acceptance or rejection of Paul's words. One contemporary moral attitude maintains that man in his present circumstances is too weak to avoid sin. His job, his neighbors, his family, his friends, his basic human needs and drives—all these account for his failure to live by the law of charity and justice.

The attitude is not new. It prompted Shakespeare to write, "The fault, dear Brutus, is not in our stars, but in ourselves that we are underlings." Any truly tragic hero in drama is tragic precisely because he freely chose a course of action that led to his downfall; if circumstances had forced him, he could hardly be judged heroic. Yet man still continues in our enlightened age to excuse himself because of extrinsic factors. I recall a comic strip that depicted a wife returning in the family car from the cleaners with her husband's suit. Unfortunately, she hit a tree and wrecked the car. Confronted by her husband, she defended herself by saying, "If I didn't have to get your suit at the cleaners, I wouldn't have been driving the car." Like the child who, after spilling two glasses of milk because of his clumsiness, says, "Mommy, give me water; the milk spills."

It's not at all rare for an undergraduate to declare that his own self-interest prompted an action judged immoral according to a Christian code. Yet Christian self-interest is misunderstood if considered without any relation to God. When man is confronted with a tax increase on his property, how does his self-interest respond? Does he respond as a property owner, or as a parent wanting better schools, or as a Democrat, or as a Republican, or as an urban dweller, or as an absentee landlord who merely wants more profit from his property? Self-interest by itself is not clear and simple. Self-interest for the Christian makes sense only if he realizes that his self-interest is best served when he acts according to God's law of charity and justice.

In the final analysis, then, the person's moral attitude toward sinful actions depends on how much he really loves God and his fellowmen, on how much he really wants to prove this love by obeying God's law, on how much he will acknowledge God by proper worship of him in the offering of the sacrifice. It is proper that the Christian realize his weakness, that he know his circumstances, that he understand fully the implications of the term *self-interest*. The Christian must convince himself that he can overcome temptation, that he can surmount adverse circumstances, that he can conquer selfishness, if he wants to. If we accept Paul's words on this subject, we realize that we shall not be tempted beyond our moral strength. Circumstances need not totally overwhelm man; selfishness need not be man's sole moral guide.

Contemporary man must respond differently from ancient peoples; his response must be a response of love—a response, as Paul reminds the people of Corinth, that the ancient Israelites failed to give to God. A response of love depends fundamentally on willingness, on man's genuinely wanting to love.

The choice rests in man's hands. Clearly his failure to respond properly to God's love and God's law is neither in the stars, nor in the circumstances, nor in the world, nor in the neighbor. The fault is clearly in man himself. Placing the blame elsewhere simply avoids the central issue. Progress may have been made in our world, but there is still the need for man to learn from the moral errors of the past, even the errors committed by the people of God. Paul speaks as well to man today as he did to the people of Corinth about a genuinely valid moral attitude.

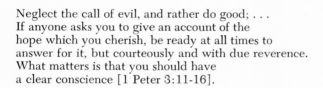

Neglect the call of evil, and rather do good; . . .
If anyone asks you to give an account of the
hope which you cherish, be ready at all times to
answer for it, but courteously and with due reverence.
What matters is that you should have
a clear conscience [1 Peter 3:11-16].

CHRISTIAN CONSCIENCE TODAY

ST. PETER reminds us of a very fundamental asser-
tion of all civilizations; namely, that good must be
done, evil must be avoided. "Neglect the call of evil,
and rather do good," says St. Peter, and he suggests
that the effects of such a procedure will be peace of
soul, the peace of a good conscience.

Men may argue about what exactly constitutes a
good act or what exactly is a bad act, but a very real
difference between good and evil has always been
accepted. Human sacrifice may be a good action to

some cultural groups; in the United States today human sacrifice is considered evil. Yet both the primitive culture and the culture of the United States make a fundamental distinction between right and wrong. The human conscience, that power within man enabling him to distinguish right from wrong, is worth consideration.

Human conscience is a power whereby man concludes that an action is good or is evil in the light of some principles. It is an intellectual activity, rooted neither in the emotions nor in the heart. A conscience must be formed and guided, the nature of fallen man being what it is, so traditionally this conscience has been formed largely by some authority —civil, ecclesiastical, or domestic. The tendency, in fact, has been to conform conscience to a law, and hence the descriptive term used today by opponents of such a procedure: the legalistic conscience.

It is this legalistic tendency that has prompted people, confronted with Christian conscience, to shout "Slavery!" For the Christian system of certain moral imperatives strikes some as intellectual enslavement, even perhaps self-torture. Perhaps the level of behavior demanded of a Christian has been thought to be too far beyond the grasp of the average Christian. In any event, a different approach to Christian conscience has been suggested. This approach is called the personal approach.

The personalistic approach to conscience is concerned, and rightly so, with the freedom conscience must enjoy. As a result of this emphasis on freedom, the personalist tends to evoke originality from the individual, even originality in moral matters. Thus the more morally original—that is, the less inhibited by law—a person is, the more freedom he will enjoy. The more freedom of conscience, the better his development as a person, because he will be acting true to himself and not true to a law.

This approach, with its emphasis on being different, on originality, on total freedom, seems somewhat sophomoric to me. I think an analogy with the history of art forms may help to illustrate why I find such an approach unconvincing. No great artist has achieved prominence because he worked in total isolation from a tradition. The great artists, the mature artists, constructed their compositions upon their predecessors and were influenced by their contemporaries. No one of the great ones felt totally free and independent of what had occurred in their chosen art medium before. Beethoven, for example, built upon Haydn and Mozart. Shakespeare borrowed heavily from his contemporaries and his predecessors. Dickens was a great storyteller, yet he really introduced little new or original into the craft of fiction; he just did it better. Thus, originality in itself, being totally different from a tradition, while it may express individuality and total freedom, does not of itself insure maturity, greatness, nor even social acceptability.

Often the personalist will say, "I feel that this action is the right one." Or "I believe that this action is good." But conscience is more than one's personal emotional response to a moral situation. Conscience is more than the attitude expressed in the words "in my heart I know I'm right."

Conscience may be either judicial or legislative. In both cases, however, conscience is an intellectual activity, not a purely personal emotional response. The judicial conscience, which was historically the conscience of the pagans, is conscience operating after an action has been performed. Man passes a moral judgment on the action: if his judgment is favorable, he enjoys peace of soul; if his judgment is unfavorable, he suffers remorse. Note that this activity of conscience is a judgment; hence an intellectual, not a purely emotional, activity.

St. Paul added a new dimension to the pagan notion of conscience, which we may call legislative. The legislative conscience directs an action prior to its being performed. This conscience must be instructed, guided, and formed according to the moral principles of the particular culture; in our situation, according to Christian principles as taught by the Church established by Jesus. The function of this conscience is to decide intelligently in advance about the moral dimensions of a situation—whether or not a particular action is good or evil; whether or not a particular action may be licitly performed.

Although others may help man form his conscience, no one may decide a question of conscience for another. Each man is responsible before God for his own acts. Not long ago a letter from a young

196

Christian couple reached me. They asked very simply, "Will you let us practice birth control?" I wrote back to them that I couldn't make that decision, that they had to decide that for themselves according to their conscience in the light of the teaching of the Church. No priest, no clergyman, can assume responsibility for another's conscience. All he can do is help form it properly according to Christian teaching on morality.

In practice, the important question regarding conscience seems to me to be this: what is the authority of conscience? Or, must I follow my conscience? Provided that the conscience is formed in good faith and on rational grounds, the authority of conscience has both a negative and a positive significance. Negative in that a man is forbidden to act against his conscience; positive in that a man is obliged to follow his own conscience. Conscience then has authority over man as the immediate criterion of his moral actions. It is not the sole criterion, however, for the remote criterion is the law itself, either revealed by God and interpreted by the Church or established by men in civil law for the proper governing of ·the people. Conscience is the immediate criterion of morality; law the remote.

Each of us has a duty to form our conscience correctly. What role, though, does ignorance play in an individual case of conscience? A person may be ignorant of a relevant fact: "But, officer, I didn't realize that I was doing eighty-five." Or he may be ignorant of a principle or a law: "But, officer, I

197

didn't know that this was a thirty-mile-an-hour zone." Finally, he may be ignorant of the sanction or punishment: "But, your honor, had I known that speeding was subject to a fifty-dollar fine, I never would have violated the law."

A further dimension of ignorance is seen in the distinction between the incorrigibly ignorant and the corrigibly ignorant conscience. The corrigibly ignorant conscience requires a simple solution: mere instruction will satisfy. But what about the incorrigibly ignorant? An individual's conscience may be incorrigibly ignorant if it never occurred to him that an important fact should be investigated; or if it never occurred to a person to question his own principles, since these same principles generally obtain in his neighborhood and among his friends; or perhaps a person's background and upbringing have conditioned him to disparage the intelligence, sincerity—yes, even the social status— of those whose principles may challenge his own.

Such incorrigible ignorance morally exonerates a man. That is, he may not be formally guilty of immorality even if his actions are wrong. Is then such a man wicked and evil? Hardly. Is he wrong? Yes, he is. Consequently, there is a need for us, particularly in our pluralistic society, to avoid judging the moral guilt of a man whose conscience does not agree with our Christian conscience.

This avoidance of judgment finds application in professional and business ethics, in private or family morality. To say, "These people deep down in their hearts know their views are wrong," is a most brash statement for a Christian to utter. On the other hand, the Christian must be careful not to violate his own Christian code merely because a majority of his friends do not accept his moral judgment. He may not act contrary to his Christian conscience merely because the neighbors think or act differently from him.

We Christians have the responsibility of forming our consciences in the light of Christian revelation, even if this revelation is unpopular among our non-Christian friends, our pseudo-Christian friends, our nominal Christian friends, and our pagan, nonreligious friends. Christian parents have the obligation to begin the formation of the proper Christian conscience in their children. And all of us need to respond wholeheartedly to Peter's imperative to "neglect the call of evil, and rather do good" for the peace of a Christian conscience is the goal and aim of our efforts.

No one must fool himself: if anyone deems himself wise by
worldly standards, he must become stupid to be really wise.
Why? Because this world's wisdom is stupidity in
God's estimate. So the Scripture says, "He catches the
wise by their cunning" [1 Corinthians 3:18-19].

THE INTELLECTUAL

AND MORALITY

CHRISTIAN MORALITY must serve man. Christian
morality must assist man to achieve his destiny.
Christian morality must enable a human being to
live in this world so that he will be able to enjoy the
reward prepared for him in the next, while at the
same time enabling him to live in this world in harmony with his civilization and with his fellowman.

If this Christian morality must serve man, the
more important question arises: whence this morality? What is this Christian morality? Is this moral

200

code entirely rooted within man himself so that man is his own moral measure?

Man himself certainly must make the decision as to when he is right and when he is wrong. As a norm to guide him, man may use a superficial code such as social protocol. In this context murder is wrong because "it is just not done"; similarly, eating peas with one's knife is wrong because "it is just not done." Society censures those who perform either action.

Or man may decide that whatever is useful to him here and now is a proper guide for his actions. For example, a student reasons that since his parents pay a telephone bill and since he is now in a telephone booth, he may remove the light fixture in said phone booth because it would be a useful bed lamp for his room in the campus residence hall.

In both these attitudes—social protocol or a thing's usefulness—the moral norm man uses is ultimately himself. Admittedly, a very simple and quite convenient norm. If man is consistent in his reasoning and in following such a norm, he will also realize that no one can really sanction anyone very seriously. No one could blame Hitler for what he did, because Hitler was merely being true to his own moral convictions. His moral guide was simply his own personal attitude toward other men. Should a man protest, however, that there are civil, positive laws which are the norms for human activity, he must still explain the authority for such laws. Should he argue that those who are governed give their consent to those governing, then he is again reduced to saying that man himself, though in this case collectively, remains the norm for moral action.

It would appear, then, that man requires a norm for his moral action above and beyond himself. There is such a source. It is God's law, a law which is interpreted for mankind throughout history by the teaching Church founded by the God-Man, Jesus Christ.

Obviously some men, even some men who wish to be called Christians, refuse to accept this norm in the practical affairs of life. In his first letter to the people of Corinth, St. Paul speaks about such people when he says, "No one must fool himself: if anyone deems himself wise by worldly standards, he must become stupid to be really wise. Why? Because this world's wisdom is stupidity in God's estimate. So the Scripture says, 'He catches the wise by their cunning [Job 5:13].'" The term *worldly wise* may suggest a man who enjoys a reputation for worldly wisdom, or it may imply a man who is wise only in worldly things—having cast off as silly, irrelevant, superstitious, or unconvincing the law of God as taught and interpreted by the teaching Church. In either case, according to St. Paul, such a worldly wise man is a fool.

"This world's wisdom is stupidity in God's estimate." The result of this worldly wisdom is either error or perplexity in matters of God and the supernatural, and this eventually leads to moral ruin. And Paul quotes from the Book of Job when he adds that God "catches the wise by their cunning," that is, in their very own craftiness. Here, then, is one reason why some professed searchers of the truth do not find any complete picture regarding man's moral life: They seek it in the wrong way, by a vain wisdom that leads them toward themselves alone and away from the source of truth, God himself.

This vain wisdom, about which St. Paul speaks, is opposed to a complete wisdom that results when man seeks truth within the framework of God's existence. This vain wisdom results from opinions about man and God, about life and moral action, which man obtains solely by his own industry, ability, and research. In this search for the truth man remains supreme, the sole norm and guide. He comes upon his own tiny bit of knowledge, which he values highly because he has learned it independently of others, by himself, without an instructor, without any institution, and, above all, without any teaching Church. It is upon these truths that the vain man relies, and he disdains anything like a divine revelation, the Scriptures, a teaching tradition, or a Church.

Really, as St. Paul points out quite clearly, such confidence in a man's own reasoning powers leads not only to pride but also to stupidity and foolishness. When this foolish attitude enters the moral area of man's life, it blinds him to a more objective norm that lies above man and outside his own mental constructs.

Often enough, too, this individualistic searcher for the truth is impatient of mystery and revelation.

He fears a teaching Church will interfere with his own intellectual advancement. Hence, he is unwilling either to consult this teaching Church or to follow her teaching. Should the moral norms established by this Church interfere with the worldly wise man, he grows angry with the Church, with official churchmen, and refuses to accept this or that teaching of the Church.

The phenomenon is hardly new. The Jews felt anger, the Greeks disdain at the doctrine of Jesus. The Jewish people required a sign according to their Messianic notions; the Greeks sought a more subtle train of thought than Christianity offered. The man nailed to the cross was not the proper sign, according to the Jews; the man nailed to the cross was not subtle enough for the Greeks. Thus, as St. Paul points out, Christ crucified was to the Jews a stumbling block, to the Greeks stupidity. It is against such stupidity, against such self-deception, against such a failure to comprehend the place of the God-Man in this world, that Paul preaches.

This false wisdom of which Paul speaks, therefore, is the belief that man's own unaided powers will bring him to full religious truth and the norms for moral rectitude. Often enough a man assumes this attitude when the world begins to open up for him, usually shortly after adolescence. Such a young man comes to distrust any extrinsic moral laws; he wishes to make his own moral judgments. He murmurs against service of God, against Christian conscience, against the truths of revelation. His doubt and his scoffing endure until they ultimately grow into skeptical arguments and assertions that could lead to apostasy. At the same time, he affects originality, he desires to appear independent in all areas of thinking, he fears to be ridiculed by his worldly friends, to be classified as a square. And all these factors combine to make him speak and think disparagingly of mystery, revelation, and anything like an objective moral teaching of the Church.

If the young undergraduate persists in this stupidity, if he fails to follow a mature search for God and morality, he becomes his own worst moral enemy. Nothing is ultimately left to him but to stumble and grope in the darkness of his own puny reason and insights. As Paul says, this man is taken in his own craftiness. His attitude resembles the judicial blindness of the Pharaoh who at length could distinguish neither light nor darkness.

The cardinal error of men blessed with superior intelligence, many of whom are found on college campuses, is to value themselves precisely because of their understanding and to look down upon lesser breeds of intellect. For them, intellect is the sole measure of praise or blame; their own intellects are their sole moral guides. They speak grandly of some norm of moral living found in such generalizations as civilization, refinement, literature, science—or merely in that general intellectual illumination that unites the gifted and talented together—while the peasants stumble blindly along, led by something called Christian revelation which the peasant in his

wretched condition can scarcely accurately comprehend or truly appreciate.

As these bright people progress in their self-
centered moral righteousness, they gradually begin
to despise authority, especially the authority of an
objectively informed conscience or of a teaching
Church. They treat any submission to an objective
norm as intellectual weakness. In fact, they find
the total Christian revelation rather intellectually
unsatisfying.

Christianity, of course, has never been intellectually satisfying. The claims of Jesus of Nazareth are
supported by his miracles, but a miracle is hardly
satisfying to our intellects, especially to the skeptical or cynical. Jesus of Nazareth did not come to
be intellectually convincing. He spoke about self-
denial and the carrying of the cross. He informed
the wealthy young man that he ought to sell his
possessions, give the money to the poor, and follow
him—but the young man was too attached to his
possessions.

Nor, for that matter, did Jesus really solve the
dilemmas presented to him. "Render, therefore, to
Caesar the things that are Caesar's, and to God the
things that are God's" is a neat antithesis, but it is
hardly satisfying intellectually. And to the Pharisees
who confronted him with the woman taken in adultery, Jesus refused to discuss the theoretical or practical implications of the law. He merely said, "Let
the one among you who is without sin cast the first
stone at her" (John 8:7).

206

Christianity does have a rational basis, but in all its elements, and particularly in Jesus' own life, it is not intellectually satisfying. In searching for a moral norm that will be personally satisfying to their own intellects, some Christian intellectuals resemble those people who, after Jesus had spoken, merely shook their heads, said "These are indeed hard sayings," turned away, and walked with him no more.

The Christian intellectual, the searcher for the truth, the young undergraduate, must decide for himself whether his norm for moral action will be his own personal intellect or whether it will be a norm that exists outside himself. The committed Christian accepts the law of God as interpreted by the teaching Church; the vaguely nominal Christian accepts his own personal reactions. In considering the option, it is wise to recall Job's words about God's trapping of the worldly wise man in his own cunning, which is another way of saying what the Psalmist sings, "The Lord knows how futile are the reasonings of the wise" (Psalms 93:11). When man becomes his own sole moral guide, how futile he becomes!

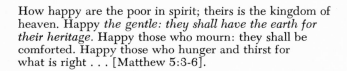

How happy are the poor in spirit; theirs is the kingdom of
heaven. Happy *the gentle: they shall have the earth for
their heritage.* Happy those who mourn: they shall be
comforted. Happy those who hunger and thirst for
what is right . . . [Matthew 5:3-6].

HAPPY ARE THEY

WHO READ

THE WISDOM a Christian should possess, although
ultimately extending itself to the supernatural and
the divine, quite definitely includes the natural and
the human. The Christian who contents himself
solely with a knowledge of apologetics, catechism
responses, and a few vocal prayers to aid his devotion, on the assumption that these alone are sufficient for growth in supernatural wisdom, assumes a
somewhat naïve position.

Catholics who send their children to Catholic
schools solely because training in prayer and teach-

208

ing about God is presented there betray only a partial understanding of Christian education. Catholic schools are hardly restricted to grading one's progress in devotion, important as devotion may be. Eucharistic processions and group worship at the beginning of the school day, which differentiate the Catholic school from the secular school, are only one element of Christian education. The entire curriculum, if properly handled, leads to a deepening of faith, hope, and charity, the theological virtues that concern man's relationship to God, to his fellowmen, and to his world.

These virtues are powers that must, like any other God-given talent, be developed by the individual person. It is perhaps anomalous that these virtues, while directly developed by prayer and contemplation, are strengthened and supported by intellectual discipline. Man develops himself by growing in knowledge, in information about himself, his neighbor, and his God; by increasing his understanding, whereby he observes the full significance of his information; and by enrichening his wisdom, wherein he sees clearly the relationships existing between his knowledge and his understanding. To achieve this intelligent wisdom, however, a Christian must read more than the catechism. So I would suggest another beatitude: "Happy the Christian who reads, for he may deepen his faith, hope, and charity."

This subject of intelligent reading has immediate pertinence because of our formal commitment in the United States to education. What the Christian ought especially to reflect upon in all this is his need to sustain the development of his mind, of his intelligence. Christian undergraduates ought to be convinced that by developing their minds during their college years they are, if properly guided, developing themselves in a fuller faith, hope, and charity. The problem is that this development must occur amid cultural elements inimical to the proper cultivation of the intellect, amid an atmosphere that may positively impede growth in faith, hope, and charity. These elements are not in themselves evil, but the concrete situation reveals that they truly are impediments at times to Christian intellectual growth.

One good example of this cultural hindrance to intellectual development through reading, an example that relates specifically to students, are the numerous "Back to School" notices in the daily papers. "First to Sears, then to School," we read, as if a large outlay of money on clothing and assorted frippery were necessary prerequisites for the learning process in college. The alliteration of the phrase so captivates our ears that we might begin to believe that a student registers for the school year at a department store.

Another retailer advertises, "Do Your Own Campus Thing." And what is this campus thing? I had always thought that it was study, reading, discussion, research in the library. But one of the local emporia informs me through their newspaper notices that it is none of these. No, doing your own campus thing pertains to selecting items from a twelve-page newspaper insert that catalogs articles any student could easily live without and still grow in wisdom.

For example, within these twelve pages there are pictured five types of slippers. "It's nice to come home to velour ballerinas for heel-to-toe cushiony comfort," is the caption describing one of them. Now I will admit that some undergraduates strike me as thinking with their feet, but I doubt if most college students feel as though they'd been on a fifty-mile hike after leisurely walking even the most expansive campus. Of another style slipper we read: "Fleece scuff soothes deliciously after dashing about days and evenings." The only dashing about on campus I know of occurs at the end of class and in the rush to the dining hall.

Within these twelve pages, moreover, are listed such other indispensable items for university education as portable vacuum cleaners, eight different types of clothes hangers, a collapsible sweater dryer, four types of garment bags, jiffy towels, an instant shoeshine kit, a case to protect your wiglet. There is also a magic turban (probably manufactured in Brooklyn, not New Delhi) to protect one's hair set, a pair of electric scissors, and a light for the closet that comes on automatically when one opens the closet door. If one has all those garment bags, of course, such a light may well be a necessity. There are some superfluities listed. Like the slim note poster and message taker upon which you can pen notes to your roommate, particularly helpful if you were not on speaking terms with him. Or if you care not for the slim note poster and message taker, there is a neat cork ball to which you can affix your notes—and it also serves as a pen and pencil holder.

This gathering of flim-flam is known, in the minds of a local merchant, as doing your campus thing. The suggestion is that all this gathering and collecting is a vital part of the educative process, part of the growth in wisdom. For some it may be the whole of their education. Nowhere in any back-to-school advertisement that I have read is there a suggestion of valuable books. It is hardly surprising that we are not a reading nation if we are content to live in the world of television, and if going to school is conditioned by the advertisements found in the daily press.

The effects of a TV-oriented world, of an education largely through the sense of sight, can be observed in some undergraduate attitudes toward the study of philosophy. A marketing major said to me not long ago, "Philosophy is just a bunch of words." The sad implication of his observation, apart from the somewhat awkward image of words appearing like grapes or radishes, is the young man's failure to realize that man lives by words. Words have conceptual significance. Words have meaning, and ultimately man penetrates the meaning of himself, of his God, of his neighbor, and of his universe through words. Words may be considered the basic way by which a man develops his mind and thereby deepens his faith, hope, and charity.

212

But if the Christian is to grow in intelligence and to deepen his faith, hope, and charity, he must live an intelligent life, and this demands reading, reflection, prayer, and contemplation. The Christian undergraduate ought not feel it a waste of time to browse in the library. The Christian ought to be eager to stroll through a bookstore looking at the recent and decent. Too many of us use a bookstore to purchase greeting cards, wrapping paper, pictures of Bogart and W. C. Fields, or any other sundry items that bookstores supply because they could not exist on their sale of books alone. In a nation that spends over eleven billion dollars a year on liquor, there is hardly any reason to plead economy. Paperbacks make excellent reading available to everyone in this country at reasonable prices. Yet not long ago I read that there are more blacksmith shops in the United States than there are bookstores. Believe it or not, in this age of the space rocket and the Mustang, it is easier to have your horse shoed than to purchase a book. Admittedly books are purchased, many for the coffee table where they become conversation pieces or part of the domestic decor, but really nobody reads them. We may collect books because every home ought to have a few, but does anyone really read them?

Though many of us will not be in classrooms this year, every Christian ought to take the slogan "Back to School" to heart and attempt to find time in a busy schedule to make room for serious reading. At least for a few evenings each week abandon the

213

tube for a good book. Substitute solid reading for the syrupy sentimentality of *Family Affair*. Buffy will hardly grow up very fast.

Books are a great gift. More importantly, reading is a necessity, not a luxury, for the Christian who wishes to stay alive and to deepen the theological virtues within himself. What a pitiable thing it is if "Back to School" means primarily gathering bric-a-brac that have nothing to do with challenging and expanding the human mind. What a sad situation results when Christians sit mesmerized before the magic lantern evening after evening at the expense of solid reading. So presumptuously, perhaps, but not without some cause, as we pray for a deepening of our faith, our hope, and our charity, let me add to Jesus' Eight Beatitudes a ninth that has contemporary relevance: "Happy the Christian who reads, for he may deepen his faith, hope, and charity."

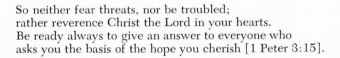

So neither fear threats, nor be troubled;
rather reverence Christ the Lord in your hearts.
Be ready always to give an answer to everyone who
asks you the basis of the hope you cherish [1 Peter 3:15].

PERSONAL PRAYER AND
SOCIAL AWARENESS

AFTER SPEAKING of the moral duties of Christians,
St. Peter in his first letter encourages his readers in
time of persecution and in a time of trouble among
the Christians themselves, "So neither fear threats,
nor be troubled; rather reverence Christ the Lord in
your hearts." This general imperative whereby Peter
calls for personal prayer could be taken to heart by
Christians today as well.

We may not be suffering persecution today as
Christians; nevertheless there are disturbing ele-

ments among Christians that parallel the disturbing factions that exist in the social and political areas of our world. And amid all the contemporary unrest and uprisings, amid the extremist movements that arise along with great social changes in any society, the Christian must make room in his life for personal prayer, for reverencing Christ in his heart. We hear so much talk these days about the social dimension of Christianity that the Christian's need for prayer can be overlooked. Yet the Christian must ever keep in mind that man reverences God not by his social actions alone but also by his personal prayer.

Our world presents such a complex situation today that only the single-minded Christian can maintain his balance, and nothing will enable a person to keep a cool head among the rising disturbances in the Church and in society today so much as prayer. Personal prayer may not offer any remedies, but it will enable the Christian to appraise the situation more calmly.

Today's new emphasis on social awareness has so influenced us all that each of us is keenly aware of the interdependence of our actions. As a recent article in the New York *Times* pointed out, we understand more clearly than ever now that none of our actions is isolated from other men. Rather amazingly, we are just beginning to realize that those who have power and financial resources in this world are inextricably linked to the disadvantaged, to those who do not. We are gradually learning that it is impossible to maintain suburban homogeneity and yet attain integrated communities simultaneously. We are slowly realizing that part of the wealth of New York and Pittsburgh and Cincinnati depends on the mining of cheap Appalachian coal and the exploitation of the poor. We are beginning to realize that California wines are possible because of the sweat of underpaid migrant workers, that it is impossible under existing practices to use schools and colleges as instruments to select some youth for later economic advancement without using the same schools to reject others.

Together with this new social awareness goes an acceptance of the young person in society to an extent greater than in any previous era. When I say that, I do not mean the whole platform of clichés referring to student uprisings, LSD, premarital sex, hippies, the Rolling Stones and the Loving Spoonful, and other groups that make some of us curse the invention of electricity. I mean more basically that, perhaps for the first time, many Americans are clearly looking to the young people, not to the older folk. This is the fact today. America is more than bemused by its youth. It is led by its youth. Read any newspaper and see the amount of news being made by those under the age of thirty.

Young people throughout history have always been in the vanguard of reform and revolution, but in America, at least, they have tended to carry someone else's banner; they were doing someone else's thing. Now they are doing their own thing. Today's young people—blacks in the urban areas, whites in the suburbs, the college students, the peaceniks—all are looked upon as the initiators and inventors of ferment, of change, and of rebellion. Many kids today are growing up to be the kind of kids their parents wouldn't have let them play with.

With youth as central to contemporary American life goes a further consideration. Whether it is unpatriotic to suggest that America is a sick society may be a moot point. The fact is, however, that "we got problems." Anywhere one goes in America today he sees manifestations of social change and social disorder, of dislocation and of reform.

Now the Christian will live amid such situations not with any handy-dandy, do-it-yourself-manual plan; Christianity does not spell things out specifically. The Christian must rely on his own social awareness. But more for his own sanity and for his own perseverance as a Christian, he must pray. He must revere Christ in his heart amid the surging problems—and for those over thirty, among a hostile opposition.

The Christian, while working according to his ability and his circumstances to bring about greater social awareness—both in himself and in others—does so fully cognizant that this world is not a lasting city. The pseudoprophet tries to tell man that he must build a type of Jesus utopia in this world, whether it's the inner city or the outer city, that the goal of Christianity is one huge earthly Christmas tree with presents underneath for everybody. The

Christian knows better. He knows that the culminating mystery of Christ's earthly life was Calvary, not Christmas.

Yet that knowledge does not lead the Christian to despair of this life, nor to be fearful of tomorrow. The prayerful Christian has no need to fear as long as he continues to pray. He may not understand clearly, but he still trusts God. Christianity, if it offers anything, offers us hope; and because of hope, Peter can well remind Christians not to fear. And hope leads us to prayer.

Without prayer today, man could easily become as cynical as our so-called sick comedians. It would admittedly be easy for the over-thirty folks to be cynical about this Pepsi generation that is running the nation with its naïve and superficial attitude toward love. Like steam heat, love keeps teenyboppers warm, even though it's ninety percent hot air. But the cynical approach, though so very tempting to all of us over thirty, leads ultimately nowhere.

So there is need for Christians to give themselves to prayer unreservedly. Some pray better than others, perhaps, but all must pray to God. There is a vast difference between losing because we didn't succeed and losing because we never tried. There is no need, as Peter says, for Christians in a schizophrenic age like ours to worry or to fear. There is a need, as Peter reminds us, to reverence Christ in our hearts, to turn to God in prayer. Only in this way will we keep the balance we need amid the kaleidoscopic events around us.

My advice is that, first of all, there should be
prayers offered for everyone—petitions, intercessions and
thanksgiving [1 Timothy 2:1].

PRAYER PUTS IT TOGETHER

ST. PAUL in his letter to Timothy urges prayer as a
necessary condition for any Christian. Prayer, we
were taught, is the raising of the mind and the heart
to God. Should this catechism description sound too
ethereal for you, then consider prayer as the voice
of man's desires. Such prayer, even if answered, will
not totally fulfill man, for man's heart is made to be
restless until it finally rests in God. Yet prayer, this
voice of desire, supports a person's religious life;

220

contemplation lies behind the intelligent life. If a man is to exercise his creativity, if he is to develop wisdom, if he is to grow aware of himself in this world, then he needs quiet reflection. He needs, in other words, prayer. Prayer, intelligent reflection, wisdom, religion—they are all clearly interrelated.

Moses Herzog, Saul Bellow's hero, declares that what America needs is a good five-cent synthesis. Could man purchase such a synthesis, wisdom would be as readily available as toothpaste. Unfortunately, wisdom comes as no economic bargain.

Man therefore searches for a synthesis in varied ways and in different places. Many of these ways relate only extrinsically to man. An advertisement in the New York *Times* magazine, for example, recently declared: "Hudson Brings Your Bathroom Together." Whether the water closet looms large among man's priorities may be a moot point, but this theatrical declaration illustrates a common misapprehension: namely, that something extrinsic to man can guarantee synthesis, can bring it all together. A naïve soul like myself, were he to realize that his bathroom was torn asunder, would likely invoke the aid of a plumber. But in this ad I am told that I can put it all together merely by purchasing facial tissue and bathroom tissue that match. Significantly, the product's name is Together.

It is amazing what problems are solved by Together. "Together . . . ends the drag of hunting around for facial tissues and bathroom tissue that actually match," reads the advertisement. One queries whether the quest for these domestic items is really a drag. An analogy with the Holy Grail rises to my mind. For the past twenty-seven years I have been spoiled; the quest for blending tissues has always been someone else's drag.

Together does even more. "It also takes care of that other tiny problem: where to put the spare roll of bathroom tissue." Amid the current domestic chaos in America, it is indeed consoling to realize that this problem, albeit a tiny one, admits of solution. Have we become so materialistic that toilet paper—pardon me, bathroom tissue—has become a vital issue? Can housewives truly achieve synthesis if only they can match the tissues in their baths? Well my point, in any event, is that here in the promise of this advertisement the achieved synthesis has nothing to do with the inner man; it is purely extrinsic.

Today's cry, "Let's get it all together," rings hollow unless a substantial internal force is at work; mere extrinsic factors do not and cannot effect synthesis. A compost pile has it all together, but its unity hardly resembles the synthesis necessary for intelligent human living. One hardly achieves synthesis through addition and multiplication of things. Synthesis, in fact, may depend on subtraction and division. Piling one item atop another proves man's avarice; it does not indicate an interior unity of spirit. Fools collect; the wise man chooses. And choice depends on an interior religious synthesis, which is supported by prayer.

There are certain cultural aspects of twentieth-century America that help to frustrate this prayerful synthesis which the Christian needs. We Americans, for example, believe as a group that acquiring things indicates advancement. The more we have, the better persons we are. It takes prayerful consideration to eliminate the superfluous from our lives. Four years ago my library consisted of about seven hundred books, most of which pertained to literature. "Why do I keep them," I thought. Simply because I felt I needed them for my work. After some consideration, I gave them to the McDonald Library. In the years since then do you know how many of those books I have had to withdraw from the library? Exactly five. Yet I could deceive myself that absolutely every single one of them was vital to my teaching. Acquiring does not imply growth.

Yet our absurd American life-style, perhaps the life-style of western man generally, continues to hinder spiritual growth and prayer. In the *New York Review of Books* recently there appeared among the advertisements this imperative: "Phase out sandboxes. Teach your cat to use the bathroom." I apologize for the several cloacal references, but this advertisement syndromatically reveals American absurdity. Cats are as important as people; acquisition more convincing than contemplation.

Walker Percy's latest novel, *Love in the Ruins*, which appears to be an extension of the thesis in Joseph Heller's absurd *Catch-22*, expresses an apocalyptic vision—his subtitle is: "The Adventures of a

Bad Catholic at a Time Near the End of the World."
Dr. Thomas More, rifle in hand, surveys from the
cloverleaf of dissecting interstate highways in Louisiana the ruins of a Howard Johnson motel, symbol of the decay of the American dream. That
gives you the idea. The novel's religious absurdity
is revealed in Percy's triple division of the Catholic
Church: (1) the American Catholic Church with
headquarters in Cicero, Illinois; (2) the Dutch
Church which believes in relevance, but not in God;
(3) the Roman Catholic remnant, a tiny, scattered
flock with no place to go.

Percy's vision is simultaneously humorous and
terrifying. One line in the book crystalizes the situation very neatly. For author Percy concludes that
what finally destroyed America was not communism,
not any invading army, but simply "that things
stopped working and nobody wanted to be a repair-
man." Here is absurdity, surely. It suggests a paraphrase of W. S. Gilbert's line, "When everyone's
somebody then no one's anybody." The notion of
equal materialistic opportunity for all leads in this
direction. A democracy predicated on a consumer's
market alone is doomed. If the morally virtuous life
is lacking—and prayer is as necessary for such a virtuous life as fresh air is for breathing—then a culture
becomes absurd.

Absurdity has led us to the point where nothing
shocks us any longer. Sin hardly startles us, because
the psychologists and the youthful gurus have urged
that there is no such thing as sin. Every man simply

does his own thing. Tragedy hasn't existed in the western world since the Elizabethans; not even televised melodrama startles us, because we view the pathos and the chaos, the depravity and the crime, the stupidity and the absurdity of all mankind on the six o'clock news. We have no need for theater after that.

There are other elements in today's world which prevent a prayer life, which impede that contemplation to which St. Paul urges us. The information syndrome, for instance. "How To Give Your Child a Superior Mind," read a notice in last week's *Book World*, found in the Chicago *Tribune*, self-styled "World's Greatest Newspaper" (how unegalitarian). One learns from this notice that a superior mind is one to whose IQ thirty points may be added. Now performing such a feat may guarantee admission to the proper Ivy League college—another unegalitarian syndrome in our democracy—but a high IQ in itself hardly guarantees growth in wisdom. No IQ examination tests one's contemplative spirit which leads to wisdom. And if I may be permitted a blunt aside, there are brilliant persons with extremely high IQs abroad in this world who show less wisdom than a blind mule.

Finally there is the cult of youth which surrounds us. Their apologists say: "Youth may be rash and clumsy in their efforts, but they are trying to tell us something." No one knows better than a teacher of English at Xavier how these young people are trying to articulate a position. Basically, though, what is so new about telling us we are living in an absurd, mixed-up world? Amos and Osee said the same thing—and I might add with more verve and clarity than some under-thirties—centuries ago.

Yet the notion that the under-thirties have a corner on wisdom spreads daily. Simply because they are under thirty seems to qualify them to represent all that is good and true and beautiful and, especially, creative. I react strongly. Yes, I root for the Oakland Raiders; any team in this day and age willing to carry a forty-five-year-old quarterback can't be all bad.

The cult of youth leads to a prejudice against older persons. A lecherous person over thirty is a dirty old man; under thirty, he's a swinger. Each week the local newspapers have Youth sections for teen-agers. How about something like the "Gerontology Roundup," a weekly review for all us folks creeping up on senility? And wouldn't the western flavor of that title captivate those who identify with Matt Dillon and Hoss?

All these absurd elements in American culture aren't about to go away. There is little hope of changing the situation, so we had best adjust ourselves through prayer and quiet reflection to live sanely in an insane world. Avarice, impulse buying, acquisitiveness, will prevail as long as man is fallen man. The compiler of facts rather than the true student will be lauded by academic leaders. College Board scores will continue to loom more significant than wisdom. Man will continue to identify each

226

and every change with progress. Above all, youth will prevail. They have the game plan. Until parents cut off their allowances, we oldsters can only plead for mercy.

Let's then face the facts. We cannot turn this absurd world around, we can only turn ourselves around. We can follow Paul's advice about prayer. We can pause during the day for something more than a coke. Perhaps we won't accept the necessity of prayer until we realize what our ultimate destination in this world is. That schoolmarm in the film *Spencer's Mountain*—don't see it: it has less vitality than *As the World Turns*—says very well: "The world steps aside to let any man pass if he knows where he's going." The wise Christian who prays knows where he's going, even if the world around him remains absurdly and unwisely in the dark.

Heaven and earth will pass away,
but my words will never pass away.
But as for that day and hour, nobody knows it, . . .
So stay awake, because you do not know the day when
your master is coming [Matthew 24:35-42].

MAN'S STATUS

IN THE TWENTY-FOURTH chapter of St. Matthew's
Gospel, two events are foretold and one is implied:
the destruction of Jerusalem and the coming of the
Son of Man are foretold by our Lord, with their implications for the end of the world and the last judgment. The passage reminds us that we are all
working toward some final goal that will all be completed and fulfilled one day in Christ. The corollary
of this, of course, is that this world is not lasting;
man is not supreme.

228

Recent history, though, has shown man rather optimistic about his own fulfillment and development without Christ. Ever since democracy replaced monarchy in the western world, ever since the romantic movement reacted to the somewhat hollow rules of neoclassicism, man has felt obliged to dispense with the chains that had been forged (so many felt) by the God of institutional religion.

This phenomenon found expression in Protestantism during the nineteenth century; Catholics have only directly experienced the effects of this attitude in the past several years. But the romantic optimist's creed, which neatly coincides at many points with the dogma of the agnostic humanist, was crystalized in the Humanist Manifesto that emanated from Antioch College in 1934. Man, it said, was infinitely capable of his own completion, his own perfection, his own self-fulfillment; man had need neither for grace nor religion nor God nor church affiliation to perfect himself.

One fact of later human history somewhat destroyed this illusion: the atomic bomb. Man proved he had great power by harnessing the atom; the difficulty was that, as with most inventions, some evil was present. Man, by proving his power, planted the seed of his own destruction. So the humanist agnostic and the romantic optimist came up with a new approach: man would find himself in his own existential environment, which demanded that there be some type of universal brotherhood of love—naturally without the fatherhood of God, for this was a man-oriented world where God really had no position.

A piece by Philip Toynbee in the London *Observer* illustrates the problem that confronts the humanist agnostic and the romantic optimist. Man must "pay fitting respect to the commonplace and the everyday," writes Toynbee. And again, there must be a "determination to take risks in order to restore man to his true stature." We are witnessing today this enthronement of the commonplace. Our sentimental literature and TV drama center upon Jake and Minnie in their Brooklyn flat working out their salvation and happiness without God, and without even much respect for the neighbor. Democratic man, influenced by romanticism, is attempting to elevate himself by ironically taking the very pedestrian and the very minimal as his norm, as the best against which all else is measured.

The error made by the humanist agnostic and the romantic optimist is fundamentally that we have here on earth a lasting city—something Jesus warns us clearly against in this section of Matthew's Gospel. Moreover, the agnostic attempts to restore man's basic dignity through everyday experience, whereas man already has an ontological dignity that arises from the God in whose image he was made. There is nothing sacred about the secular in itself, nothing sublime about the pedestrian, nothing extraordinary about the trite, unless man realizes that these things have value in view of the very source of life, God himself.

When man becomes aware of the coming of the Son of Man and of the fulfillment of the kingdom of God, he comprehends the need of working toward God through the commonplace and the everyday.

Man will restore himself to his proper stature not by falsely identifying the commonplace with the eternal, but by acknowledging that one day this commonplace, which confronts him and which he accepts and uses properly, will pass away. Man's true stature will be restored only when man recognizes his true position in the hierarchy of a universe that is part of God's world.

The various love movements, the hippie movement, the "Gentle Tuesday" movements—all of which tend to canonize the commonplace and to metamorphose at times the sordid into the sublime, the trivial into the ecstatic, even the immoral into the moral— these movements will spend themselves. Men must either accept God's warning of the transiency of this life, or men will vainly attempt to build on earth a lasting city without God, as the agnostic humanists and the optimistic romantics attempt.

The prophetic words of Jesus make sense to the believer. To the cynic, the skeptic, the agnostic they are but hollow, highly imaginative words exploited by churchmen to frighten man into a stupid submission against which he instinctively rebels. But I think it must amuse God to watch his sometimes rather romantic creatures in their poignant efforts to raise themselves to a status they cannot possibly achieve: man trying to become God.

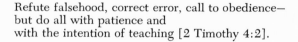

Refute falsehood, correct error, call to obedience—
but do all with patience and
with the intention of teaching [2 Timothy 4:2].

DAILY BREAD OR

DAILY SURREALISM?

THE ATTITUDES of Aquarians are often idealistic, which is admirable; they are also inclined to be utopian, which is unreal. Although they are self-styled altruists, Aquarians can develop a self-centeredness inclined toward self-contemplation that leads only to an identity crisis. Aquarians have great intellectual potential, but sloth often victimizes their efforts. Aquarians also pride themselves on mobility, whereby they ironically act as the coolest of the cool in a so-called committed generation.

232

Paul's letter to Timothy lacks appeal for Aquarians because Paul emphasizes the absolute word of God which, as Paul forecasts, will be replaced in minds and hearts by novelties, fables, myths—by anything different. "The time is sure to come," he writes, "when, far from being content with sound teaching, people will be avid for the latest novelty and collect themselves a whole series of teachers according to their own tastes; and then, instead of listening to the truth, they will turn to myths" (2 Timothy 4:3-4).

Aquarians reject the harsh words of the Bible. This rejection of the Bible, especially of the stark doctrines of the Old Testament, echoes the ancient Gnostic heresy. So does their propensity to bleed the vital ambiguity from a word like *love* and reduce it to mere sensuous relationships with other men and with the universe in general. In his recent book, *The End of Religion*, Dom Aelred Graham, the Benedictine scholar, speaks about the roots of Gnosticism found in the pre-Christian era of the first and second centuries before Jesus. His summary of Gnostic doctrines surely anticipates the views of Aquarians in A.D. 1970:

Chief among the objections to Gnostic thought were that it taught the existence of a higher God than the one who created the world, that it drew a distinction between the Creator and Redeemer, that it repudiated the Old Testament, that its docetic view of Christ eliminated him from the historic process, that it denied the Resurrection, and that its ethical teaching fluctuated between extreme asceticism and self-indulgent libertinism (p. 89).

The Gnostics aimed at direct intuition of the deity, at personal experience of the divine through the senses. Today's Gnostics, the Aquarians, seek through drugs and incense and sensitivity sessions what the Oriental attempts through contemplation. And these attitudes of Aquarians are all related: search for transcendence, rejection of time and history, elimination of an historical Jesus and especially of his teaching in the Bible.

Perhaps significantly, they find comfort in Oriental religion, at least on the superficial level, for Oriental religions also reveal little concern with what occurs in time, but only with escaping from time. Our Aquarians strive to find God outside history. As a result, they have little need for either a Bible or for an historical Jesus. At best, the Bible for them is a good book of some wisdom. Jesus at best is a greater man, in Milton's sense, or even a superstar, who struts and frets his hour upon the stage and then is heard no more.

The Aquarians' exploitation of drugs to move beyond time means they do not pray in the words our Savior taught us, "Give us this day our daily bread." One need not take *bread* in the colloquial sense of money, which Aquarians scorn (at least when others have it). *Bread* is earthy and basic and temporal.

234

The Aquarian does not want bread from God; he wants divinity itself above and beyond. He prays rather "Give us this day our daily surrealism," for something that will transport him into a vague sense of what he believes to be transcendence.

Once again, man tends toward one extreme or the other. We need not disdain an incarnate God in order to gain a share with the transcendent; nor need we reject as absurd any transcendent God for the sake of maintaining a God who walked among us. God is at once immanent, incarnate, one of us—and transcendent. Rejection of any aspect reveals an oversimplification of the notion of Christian love: love of God and love of neighbor.

But the Aquarian exploits drugs in an effort to induce artificially an experience that God alone can proffer. Timothy Leary, one of the high priests of drug cultists, has declared that LSD provides an experience comparable to the mystical graces enjoyed by Teresa of Avila. While my personal experiences can't prove him wrong, my skepticism in his analysis arises from the fact that mystical experience is a gift of God, not something achieved solely by man's efforts, with or without drugs.

Tom Wolfe, in his documentation of Ken Kesey's experiences with the Merry Pranksters, speaks of this situation. In Wolfe's book, *The Electric Kool-Aid Acid Test*, Kesey, who inspired the first communal public use of LSD on the Pacific Coast, explains that LSD shows what can be achieved. He adds a significant note, however, recorded by Tom

Wolfe, when he speaks of going "beyond acid."
Wolfe explains:

> You find what you came to find when you're on
> acid and we've got to start doing it without acid;
> there's no use opening the door and going through
> it and then always going back out again. We've
> got to move on to the next step (p. 364).

In Kesey's own analysis of that so-called transcendental experience toward which he and the Merry
Pranksters were striving, "It's not the drugs. In fact,
I'm going to tell everyone to start doing it without
the drugs." Whether Aquarians will follow this
further teaching of one of their own gurus only time
will tell.

The quest for transcendence, though, is a beautiful search if done in the proper way. There is as
much of a problem, however, with those who believe
that the total search moves on a horizontal level as
with those Aquarians who proceed awkwardly
through the artificial, like drugs. This morning,
while listening to the words of Archbishop Leibold
on television, I was struck by his comparison of our
renewal in the Church, concretely realized here in
Cincinnati through the Synod, as a second Pentecost. The archbishop declared it is time for us to
"leave the upper room," the scene of the first Pentecost; his metaphor indicates that we must go where
the action is. Perhaps I speak from a cynical disposition; perhaps from personal failure. With all due respect to the archbishop, I think the problem is less

with leaving the upper room for involved Christian activity—necessary as that may prove—than it is with remaining in the upper room. Not to pop pills or shoot drugs, but to pray and to contemplate, to study and to read, to listen and to hear.

The Christian's tendency today leads him out of that upper room whither the Spirit came. He tends to look for his God in things. The Aquarians, though their methods are suspect, are proceeding in a manner the twentieth-century Christian very much needs to follow. Only instead of using drugs as a surrogate for prayer and quiet reflection, let the Aquarian follow the route of Paul's advice to Timothy: turn toward history, toward time, toward the Bible where we find the real Jesus.

The urge to leave the upper room seems especially strong these days among clergy and seminarians. In their efforts to be relevant, they often make some interesting choices. Rev. Jerry Ward of International Falls, Minnesota, races stock cars in his spare time. Painted on the side of his racer are the words: "The Honking Padre." Sounds like a goose. His motives are lofty enough: "I must go where the people are," he says, "and there are a lot of people connected with stock-car racing." True, but is a mere congregation of people the sole criterion? It may be a good one, but hardly the sole reason for the choice of apostolate. I enjoy the horses, but I wouldn't paint on the side of a Xavier University car: "The River Downs Padre." And I know there are a lot of people connected with organized crime, but I am hesitant about submitting an application to be chaplain of the Mafia.

And there is more to being a Christian than merely leaving the upper room, as our archbishop suggests; we must also learn to long for the Spirit in the upper room. Among other things, this demands faithful adherence to the word of God. It is this, as Paul says to Timothy, that enables the "man who is dedicated to God [to become] fully equipped and ready for any good work" (2 Timothy 3:17). To do such work, the Christian needs the daily bread of prayer and contemplation, he needs to accept an actual world into which God actually came. He does not need to assume a surrealistic attitude that in its naïveté strives to find God in a way difficult to square with the word of God. This was not the route of him who was sent to us. Nor need we search for another.

Let the message of Christ, in all its richness,
find a home with you. Teach each other, and
advise each other, in all wisdom. With gratitude in
your hearts sing psalms and hymns and inspired
songs to God; and never say or do anything except in the
name of the Lord Jesus, giving thanks to
God the Father through him [Colossians 3:16-17].

THE IMPROMPTU MORAL SONG

ST. PAUL exhorts Christians to follow some general
rules of Christian behavior, among which is the suggestion to assist one another through the singing of
inspired songs. His words may well refer to the
charismatic improvisations prompted by the Holy
Spirit that occurred in the early Church and perhaps occur even today. Such spontaneity, however,
does not necessarily suggest that the Christian can
be totally impromptu in his moral life. Yet anyone
even partially aware of tendencies in Christianity
today will recognize how Paul's words can be used

239

as a scriptural support for all sorts of extreme experiments performed in the name of personal, impromptu inspiration.

No one denies that the Holy Spirit inspires departures from accepted practices. The saints were hardly run-of-the-mill types. If the saints departed from the norms, though, their departures were rather in degree than in kind. The saints were not extraordinary because they dispensed with man, but because they did what an ordinary man does in an extraordinary way. It remains a risky business to claim the Holy Spirit's inspiration for moral positions that differ essentially from the word of God as presented by his teaching witness, the Church.

Christian history is full of illustrations of the danger in removing a part of the Bible's message at the expense of the whole. So Paul is not urging that man be totally impromptu in moral matters, that each man do his own thing in his own way. Paul clearly states that there are teachers to be heard, laws to be obeyed, and ordinances to be followed. And therefore if a certain moral position obviously stands at 180 degrees from the position of Christ's teaching witness, the Church, the Christian should be hard put to accept it—no matter how much personal inspiration of the Spirit an individual may claim for such a position.

This passage from St. Paul's letter ought to be kept in mind as we read articles about the contemporary moral climate in our country, about what is called the permissive generation. Admittedly, certain former taboos have today been dispelled in our society. Citizens today are more formally educated and so approach life in a more sophisticated manner than their counterparts of fifty years ago. Man must develop his own freedom, and to enable man to develop himself freely, society—ecclesiastical, domestic, and civil—must be and is more tolerant today. Above all, Church, family, and state must be especially careful not to label as immoral an action that clearly is not.

This permissiveness, however, brings with it the same risks that guidance by the Spirit brings. One comforting feature of the former method of determining right from wrong was that there was little doubt about what precisely was expected of one: black was black, white was white. With the greater freedom today has come the obvious human risk of being wrong more easily, and perhaps with even greater frequency than we might at first suspect. A man should understand permissiveness clearly before he stoutly endorses it. In the same way, before a man starts shouting that he is inspired to an untraditional mode of moral living through the inspiration of the Spirit, he had better be quite certain that it is indeed the Holy Spirit speaking to him.

Some persons today, guided by that functional old adage "if you can't beat 'em, join 'em," are willing to declare without any qualification that the new permissiveness is exactly what mankind needs. They will, consequently, concur with every aspect of permissiveness. And they will also be disinclined to investigate claims of inspiration by the Spirit, naïvely assuming that if the person claims such inspiration, the claim is ample warrant for acceptance of the fact.

Such an attitude, for example, leads people to proclaim that a college need not concern itself with anything like a moral commitment as long as that college is, individually and collectively, vaguely searching somehow or other for that elusive thing called truth. And parents need not fret if children bed down in village pads; after all, it's the done thing. Or, as the permissive mother put it at the local PTA meeting: "My son cannot be all that bad. Why, he still loves peanut butter."

Schools and parents sometimes tend to join the teeny-boppers and the college jet set in the hopes of winning them over through identification. Their hope is somehow, in this way, to bridge the generation gap. So Dad becomes a pal; Mom is a perpetual den mother; teachers who are fortunate enough let their hair grow long.

A recent Broadway play, *What Did We Do Wrong?* illustrates what occurs when this approach is followed. Enter a young man with full beard, long hair, and dirty trousers protesting against the world in general and against his college administration in particular. His father tries to reason with him. "After all," Dad says, "I didn't send you away to college to learn a lot of dirty words you could have learned here at home." But after he has spent the whole first act berating the permissive younger generation, Dad joins the younger set and later, when he appears like one of them, the audience laughs. When the parents in the audience return home to their children, though, it is a moot point whether they will still be laughing.

Permissiveness may be here to stay. At least there is not much sense waiting for it to go away. Nothing is solved, however, by Christians joining the movement. For the Ten Commandments, unfashionable as they may seem to some, have not been abrogated. No one may legitimately invoke the Second Vatican Council as having approved lying, stealing, detraction, uncharitableness, fornication, violation of the rights of others, envy, and murder. Despite the efforts of our permissive society to invoke the inspiration of the Spirit in order to convince the rest of us that immoral behavior is really moral, God's law still binds man, no matter how many people may wish to transgress it in the name of personal inspiration or self-fulfillment.

Christians, let it be remembered, by their very profession ought to differ from their unbelieving neighbors. Knowing when and where to conform and when and where to rebel demands assistance from the Spirit, as St. Paul suggests, and though it may be difficult to discern the actual operation of the Spirit within an individual soul, it seems unlikely there is much charismatic quality about many of the impoverished moral tunes being hummed by some members of our permissive American society today.

I think that what we suffer in this life can
never be compared to the glory, as yet unrevealed,
which is waiting for us [Romans 8:18].

THE CHRISTIAN AND

FORTITUDE

AMONG THE SUFFERINGS we all experience in this
life is the sense of failure, yet one of the most difficult
accommodations for any man to make is learning to
accept failure gracefully. The young Christian, especially, is inept at living with setbacks or difficulties;
he finds it awkward to admit error, or to put up with
his own lack of success. Even when the blame falls
squarely on his own shoulders, and he fully realizes
it, many a man grows bitter or discouraged or even
enraged at his inability to succeed. His world comes

244

crashing down around him, and he sees no prospects for a brighter future.

No one strives to be a loser, and yet no one can win every game. Even apparently successful men have encountered personal defeats and losses. The Christian cannot eliminate failure and suffering from his life; he should, therefore, sharpen his vision and learn to see there is more significance to life than success. In the world's eyes, Christ was never more a loser than when he hung upon the cross, and yet it was through this apparent defeat that victory came.

The Christian, like any man, is confronted with decision-making: choice of education, choice of business, choice of neighborhood, choice of home. In every decision there are pros and cons. Any decision demands some self-denial, and it is precisely here the unchristian man rebels. He will choose nothing that means denial of his whims. The genuine Christian chooses courageously. He uses his intellect, he follows his conscience. Nevertheless, that does not make his decision easy, nor does the actual choice insure success.

Christianity is constructed of hard sayings, but a Christian who genuinely wishes to follow the ethic of Jesus will live by those hard sayings. No one says that Christianity makes decisions easier; no one declares that Christianity removes all suffering; no one foolishly says that Christianity solves all hang-ups. Hang-ups are a part of life, and those who wish to eliminate such impediments are silly and naïve.

Furthermore, they do not comprehend Christianity. Jesus offers a way of life that leads to total completion and fulfillment only after this life has been completed, and thus Paul writes to the Romans that he counts the sufferings of this life as hardly worthy of comparison to the total self-fulfillment in the next life.

Our contemporary situation, with its emphasis on compromise, militates against the development of fortitude. Compromise may not destroy fortitude, but it does make the practice more difficult. Christians today are asked by some leaders to compromise with a worldly standard, to meet Satan on Satan's terms, to destroy the sacred, or at least to substitute the secular for the sacred. Some prophetic voices cry that there should be peaceful coexistence with immorality. Permissiveness has some merit, but it often implies that a man choose without any moral direction or guide, and this can be fatal. Permissiveness, also, leads to a compromise that makes the development of the virtue of fortitude almost impossible.

Certain approaches to ecumenism can serve to illustrate the world of compromise in which we live. The Disciples of Christ, some say, would join with Catholics if the organ were eliminated from Catholic churches. Or, Lutherans would be happier with Catholicism if the real presence of Jesus in the Eucharist were denied. Or, the Episcopal Church would be on pleasant terms with Catholicism if the role of Mary were diminished. Deny the efficacy of the sacrifice of the Mass, and Methodists could live with the Church; eliminate priesthood, and the Presbyterians would be content with Catholicism; the Orthodox Churches would welcome an elimination of Peter's primacy.

This is hardly ecumenism. It is rather an abandonment of doctrine for the sake of appealing to certain people. It is compromise for the sake of compromise. Surely charity and justice must be shown to all men, but an elimination of beliefs and a watering down of doctrine was hardly the approach of Jesus. Indeed, his insistence upon certain teachings drove away many springtime followers. Christians may live on friendly terms with communists, perhaps, but they cannot and need not accept their ideas about God, the Church, the state, and education. Christians who want simply to compromise with the world hardly develop the virtue of fortitude.

The fainthearted Christian is far too fond of quoting Paul's famous words about "another law in his members" that prevents his doing the good he sees and approves. Occasionally, too, such a Christian will say that he would be less a coward if only circumstances were different. But the man who blames circumstances for his lack of courage resembles the couple who grew tired of their home and wished to move to a new place. In an effort to sell their house, they wrote an advertisement for the local newspaper: "For sale: lovely ranch-style home; three bedrooms; fully equipped electrical kitchen; large dining room; spacious living room; two bathrooms; lovely garden with patio for outdoor dining; ample lawn in front." That Sunday the husband read the description to his wife who suddenly declared: "Why, darling, that sounds exactly like the type of place we're looking for!" Present circumstances are as conducive to man's development of his fortitude as any other circumstances. Man's failure to be brave is not easily ascribed to circumstances.

No, the Christian says, but he is weak. Precisely the point. It is the weak person alone who can be courageous and brave. Man is vulnerable in this life, and because he is vulnerable, he can exercise fortitude. If man were not vulnerable, he would have no need for developing fortitude. An angel is not brave; a giant is not brave; a bully is not brave. Only the weak and vulnerable can be truly courageous. Because a man's moral choices could cause him pain and anguish, he can practice the virtue of fortitude. Fortitude enables a man to face injury, to meet disappointment, to accept failure, to rejoice amid suffering.

The Christian may well ask himself, "Am I likely to be hurt by this decision?" And the answer may well come back, "Yes, you are likely to suffer from this decision." The genuine Christian will accept the possibility, and the probability, and he will make his decision realizing that he can squarely face the resulting situation because he has within him the power to be courageous, the ability to be brave—the virtue of fortitude.

LIKE TAXES, DEATH

This, then, is what I pray, kneeling before the Father,
from whom every family, whether spiritual or natural,
takes its name: Out of his infinite glory, may he
give you the power through his Spirit for your hidden
self to grow strong, so that Christ may live in your
hearts through faith, and then, planted in love and
built on love, you will with all the saints have
strength to grasp the breadth and the length,
the height and the depth [Ephesians 3:14-18].

CHRISTIAN DEATH

PAUL prays for man's spiritual growth, which enables the Christian to accept the richness of the
mystery whereby man shares the life of Christ. Yet
life in this world reveals only traces of this mystery
and this spiritual life. Complete understanding and
final sharing is found only after death, the door
through which we enter fully into the life of the
Spirit. So the spiritual growth of which Paul speaks
must somehow prepare man for that death which
leads to total happiness and self-fulfillment. Any

251

concern with the life of the Spirit, then, must include a Christian consideration of death.

Death, though, is such a commonplace among men that it tends toward the prosaic. And the more prosaic an event is, the more difficult it is to transfigure it. Indeed, Shakespeare's genius lies partially in his ability to weave a most exquisite human tapestry from greed, injustice, envy, pride—those vices of men that are as trite as the air we breathe.

When personally considered, of course, death is hardly a prosaic matter. Nevertheless its very imminence leads man to a somewhat blasé acceptance of its actuality. In his naïveté, man often likes to lead himself to think that death happens largely to other people. And when death comes to the incurably sick person, men often speak of its arrival as a merciful release. But death at any time is a release, for death frees a man from the trap of this world. This universe, for all its beauty, is a snare, and only death can free us from it. Death is really man's hope, man's salvation.

Our universe consists of fallen men who have attempted throughout history to erect a structure within which their fellowmen can live. Yet these very necessary structures, ironically, can trap a man. The great snare today in our country, as syndicated columnists often remind us, is laid by politicians, commercial leaders, and militarists, who dictate our lives in every detail, from what we watch on television to higher education. The men involved have a very simple view of life: possess everything. They cultivate avarice as an obsessive hobby. Sell Cincinnati. Buy Chicago. Pollute Lake Erie. Their decisions, while satisfying to their peers, while comforting to financiers, while catering to the egos of business and commerce, imprison the philosopher, the humanist, and—even if he may not realize it— the man on the street. No wonder the academic world is fed up.

Man is even entertained by the world of commerce, as we watch the commercial half-truths. Gillette Rapid Shave, we are told, has K34. We are not told the essence of K34, but we accept it as a good thing because Gillette entertains us. And our hierarchy of values can be controlled by commerce. Arrid stops wetness, they tell us dramatically, as if the priority of stoppages in this country would list wetness as number one. The commercial world and its satellites in advertising literally lie to us about life. They make us think we have here, in this world, a lasting city.

Our politicians and militarists concur, when they choose any means to protect "the American way," even if it means exploiting college campuses for reserve officer training programs. Propaganda replaces information. Watch your little brother in the sixth grade after he finishes playing with his toy M16 rifle and starts to write his essay for history class. You can see how he has been trapped already. He dutifully writes what he has been told to write, that, for example, the United States fought a war in 1898 to set the poor Cubans free from tyranny. During

his essay he'll add that the United States traditionally fights on the side of justice and freedom, and
therefore always wins. He may even have the te-
merity to add, "just like today in Vietnam."

The commercial world has your brother right
where they want him. The advertising world has
him right where they want him. The politicians
have him right where they want him. And the military has him right where they want him. The American structure already has your little brother's mind
and soul; when he's eighteen they'll take his body.
He has never learned to think; perhaps he never
will. He will be unsympathetic to the mystery or to
the Spirit because he has accepted the notion that
this world is all there is, that death, far from being a
beginning, is in reality the end. This world has him
imprisoned.

Let's face it, then. This life is a trap, a snare, a
huge net. Only death sets us free. Unless death conditions our personal choices, we live amid our plastic situation as a prisoner in a cell; should we
attempt to fight the system, we run our heads into
a wall. When our young men speak of love, they
are the prey of the contemporary Venus, the vinyl
woman of twentieth-century America whose prefab
sexiness is embellished by more than forty shades of
lipstick which American commerce has provided for
her. And advertising convinces her that capitalism
must be the best of all possible systems because in
a socialist country she wouldn't have such a wide
variety of choices.

Listen, we hear it said, if you don't love America, leave it. That's what we read on the bumper stickers. Yet here again is a trap. Drop out of the college structure and you're drafted. Fail to gain a degree and you push a broom for the rest of your life. Unless you take all the required courses established by the state, you may not teach on the secondary level no matter how intelligent you are. You have to "make it" to obtain what you want, but the problem is that to make it you have to live in the structural maze erected by commerce, the state, and the military.

Our desires are all neatly programmed for us by our world. Business and commerce tell us what we should like. This is life, we are told. If man takes only the existential view of life, he sees only the trap, the snare. Like Vladimir and Estrogen, man waits for Godot without knowing who Godot is, or even what he is.

The Christian waits, too, for death. But he does so eagerly because he realizes that death is the moment of victory, of release from the snare that is this life. In death the Christian finally confronts personally that Christ whom he has met before only sacramentally—and it is for this reason St. Paul talks quite literally about Christians being baptized into death. To consider death in this light, however, depends upon our growth in the Spirit.

What militates against a proper appreciation of death today is that business and politicians and the military have convinced us that we must work toward the American dream, even if in our moments of sobriety we know what a sham it is. We smile at Jay Gatsby, and yet the commercial world that controls our campuses wants us all to come out of the Midwest and make it big down East.

F. Scott Fitzgerald concludes *The Great Gatsby* with a declaration that ought to convince anyone, not totally benumbed by commerce and finance into the state of nonthink, that the American dream is one huge myth: "So we beat on, boats against the current, borne back ceaselessly into the past." For all our efforts, for all our attempts to create here a lasting secular city, for all the efforts by politicians, businessmen, and militarists to support the American dream with glib slogans, blind patriotism, and the half-truths of advertising, man realizes that he is trapped. Like Gatsby we have seen the luster of our solid-gold-Cadillac culture become slightly tarnished despite the efforts of the structure to maintain the sheen.

And so the Christian realizes that his life had better include a recognition of mystery, a spirit of contemplation, a proper place for prayer. The Christian sees the stupidity of believing, as did Jay Gatsby, in an orgiastic future that year by year recedes ironically before us. As Christians we may not abandon our environment, but we must at least recognize it for what it is.

Should the Christian fail to perceive that this world is not a lasting city, should he be unaware of the significance of death, the whole world and its full significance will elude him. He will try to run faster, to stretch his arms farther, but one fine morning he will wake to the realization that he has indeed been baptized unto death. The Christian who lives amid mystery, however, need not suffer such a rude awakening.

The error of the secular humanist is that he sees this world as both end and means. The Achilles heel of atheistic communism is that by its total commitment to this world it can find in death no more than physical decay. The Christian sees the same world, but he observes that this world is the means to God, the world transcended by the mystery that is Christ, the life of the Spirit.

Far from denying the temporal trap the world sets for man through commerce and politics and militarism, the Christian works within the confines of his earthly cell fully aware that only through this temporal existence can he reach an eternity. The Christian paradox of finding only by losing fortifies the Christian who lives largely to die. Since he has been baptized unto death, the Christian can accommodate himself to this world of commerce, politics, and militarism, and yet remain fully and forever aware that it is incomplete.

The Christian gives a prominence to death in his life because he has a spiritual vision of a time when there will be no more death, when Christ's life will be entered fully. The world of the past will one day be gone, that world of business and wars and commerce and battles and finances and skirmishes and pseudoeducators and empty politics and hollow statesmen—all will be gone. All these things are truly transient, as the primitive poets long ago realized. "Thaes ofereode, thisses swa maeg," the Old English elegiac poet declares. "That passed away, in time so will this."

Man's efforts to build a satisfying dwelling on this earth are doomed to fail. Death, toward which and into which the Christian is baptized, makes the Christian aware of his need to participate in the mystery that is Christ, to develop himself in the life of the Spirit.

All I want is to know Christ and the
power of his resurrection and to share his sufferings by
reproducing the pattern of his death. That is the way I can
hope to take my place in the resurrection of the dead.
Not that I have become perfect yet: I have not yet won,
but I am still running, trying to capture the prize for
which Christ Jesus captured me [Philippians 3:10-12].

BAPTIZED FOR DEATH

THE ELEGIAC POET expresses a longing for the past,
his thoughts ever turned toward the transiency of
life so poignantly expressed in human separation,
particularly in that permanent earthly separation we
call death. The elegiac poet mourns for himself and
for his loss. He grieves less for the departed soul
than for his own life. Human sorrow at the time of
death, real as it is, is directed ultimately toward
ourselves, not toward our beloved brother who has
died. For he has now reached not an end, but a
beginning.

259

Christian faith enables man to consider death as the very entrance into life. Death is, for the Christian, the moment toward which he lives his life and for which he prepares by sacrifice, work, charity, and justice toward his neighbor. This Christian faith is a staunch belief founded upon the person of a revealing God. It is not a misty trust in some unseen power above. Christian faith is hardly reflected in Tennyson's vague expression about God:

> We have but faith: We cannot know,
>   For knowledge is of things we see;
>   And yet we trust it comes from thee,
> A beam in darkness: let it grow.

The Christian attitude toward death is not founded upon any faint beam amid the darkness. The Christian by his very life of faith understands death as prelude to a resurrection, to a rising with Christ. By his incorporation into the life of Christ through the sacraments, the Christian veritably lives in death and for death. By his life and by his death the Christian resembles Christ, as St. Paul writes: "All I want is to know Christ and the power of his resurrection and to share his sufferings by reproducing the pattern of his death. That is the way I can hope to take my place in the resurrection of the dead."

Christian baptism plunges us literally into Christ's death, which, far from being a tragedy, is a moment of great triumph precisely because death preceded the resurrection, a promise to all faithful Christians. Scripture considers the primary effect of Christian baptism as a new life within us, but Scripture also considers that through baptism the Christian is assimilated, joined to, grafted onto Christ and Christ's death and resurrection.

In baptism, indeed, man dies to sin, a death that foreshadows his union with Christ at the moment of death. As St. Paul says to the people of Rome, "Do you not know that all of us who have been baptized into union with Christ Jesus have been baptized into union with his death? Yes, we were buried in death with him by means of baptism, in order that, just as Christ was raised from the dead by the glorious power of the Father, so we also may conduct ourselves by a new principle of life" (Romans 6:3-4).

When Paul speaks of being buried with Christ in baptism he refers to our actual death, he refers to the similarity between ourselves and Jesus Christ. Throughout his entire life a Christian dies with Christ. Through his baptism he is crucified with Christ, and the crucifixion of the Christian life is consummated in that act we call our death.

Through the Eucharist, too, the Christian celebrates the sacrificial death of Jesus Christ, a symbol of his own sacrifice and of his own death. In this sacrifice and sacrament not only is the Christian confronted by the mystery of the cross, but he is also affected by the strength communicated by the sacrifice. Christians share Christ's death because they celebrate the sacrifice and receive the sacrament of Christ's death, a sacrifice and a sacrament that is life-giving.

Thus, the Christian search for a joyful life ends at death. The Christian willingly enters this mystery that he does not fully comprehend. The mystery of faith is the mystery of life, the mystery of death. None of us can really say much about the complete human existence when its very completeness is hidden in the mystery of God.

This human existence includes our death, a mystery hidden in God. The Christian thinks of death because his life moves onward toward that moment and because death is a part of the mystery that is Jesus. Ever since Jesus died for the salvation of the world and for the full life of man, death has had joyful significance. Compared to death, all other events in a man's life are incidental, for only through the act of death does a man reach complete happiness and fulfillment.

And yet, because of the separation involved in death, man moves reluctantly toward it and resignedly accepts it. Nevertheless, because of our baptism, because of our celebration of the Eucharist, the Christian death becomes a beautiful mystery in and through Christ. Of course the agnostic smiles at Christian simplicity, at what he calls Christian naïveté. The agnostic cites the blasphemous Swinburne, in whose view man:

> Weaves and is clothed with derision,
>   Sows, and he shall not reap;
> His life is a watch or a vision
>   Between a sleep and a sleep.

The Christian rejects this agnostic position about life, since the Christian believes that through death comes joyful fulfillment. His motives for accepting such a belief are the risen Jesus in whose person he has been baptized. Death, then, prepares man for resurrection. Death is not a merciful release, but for the Christian a final action.

The departed Christian is removed from sight; he has left this world. But he has done so to live fully with the Christ in whom he has believed and whom he has willingly determined to follow. As the Jesuit poet Hopkins reminds us, this separation is not total, for "Christ minds: Christ's interest, what to avow or amend / There, eyes them, heart wants, care haunts, foot follows kind. / Their ransom, their rescue, and first, fast, last friend." To this Christ the Christian returns through his death; to a Christ who promises by his own death, to which the Christian is united, ransom, rescue, and resurrection, for by baptism and the Eucharist he is ever the Christian's first, fast, last friend.

You have been taught that when we were baptised in
Christ Jesus we were baptised in his death [Romans 6:3].

ALIVE TO GOD

ST. PAUL speaks about being baptized into death
in order to rise with Christ. Throughout this passage
from his letter to the people of Rome, the apostle
speaks both of the physical death we all must undergo and the necessary preparation for meeting
that death happily, the moral death to selfishness in
order that we may live to the charity of Christ.

As we consider the world around us and the people in it, it appears that the bland truism that each
of us must one day die makes little practical impact

on people. People seemingly give little thought to death. Of course if people do not believe in Jesus or in any afterlife, the reason for such obtuseness regarding death is clear. But if they do accept an afterlife, then it is ridiculous for people not to consider death as an important part of their lives.

The BBC some years ago telecast a program on death, and there was strong reaction from the viewers. "We don't want to see such programs; we don't want to be reminded of the fact." Yet St. Paul speaks clearly of death, not to frighten his listeners, but to give them confidence that by dying to self and living to Christ they will, like Christ, conquer death.

The thought of death can make quite a difference in our lives. The late Senator Neuberger, after he had been informed that he had six months to live, remarked how suddenly the insignificant things didn't seem to matter so much. If the biscuits were burnt, who cared? If his wife squeezed the toothpaste from the bottom of the tube while he squeezed from the top, it was hardly a federal case. The late senator said that he could no longer be bitter about anything, once he knew death was imminent.

Christians have great reason to accept death in an intelligent way. Christ has conquered death for man. Christ's death and subsequent resurrection assure us that if Christians die with him, they shall rise with him. Only Christ can give a full and complete meaning to death for the Christian, but a man will comprehend death's significance only if Christ has first given meaning to his life. Man cannot argue death out of his life. He cannot avoid death. He can prepare for death, and Paul tells us how to prepare for it: be alive to God.

Now an undergraduate may well ask, "But what does all this mean—be alive to God? How can I be alive to God? This isn't relevant to me. This doesn't reach me. This doesn't turn me on."

There seems to be a great deal of conversation today about the relevance of Christ in our world. The talk is not necessarily new; what is new is that we hear about it faster and in greater depth. Yet it is not for God to make himself relevant to us; it is for us to make ourselves relevant to him. And if the Ten Commandments, the Beatitudes, the social teaching of Jesus do not seem to reach us, it is not the fault of the doctrine; it is our fault. Each person who professes to be Christian must make Christ relevant to his life.

Perhaps we teachers have emphasized spoonfeeding a bit too much in our educational practices; perhaps we are trying to make academic subjects as palatable as possible so that knowledge won't make its proverbially bloody entrance; perhaps we have tried so hard to make students like study and to make study easy that students have begun to transfer this attitude to their moral and religious lives. As a result, if something does not really reach out and grab them like the latest pop records, they figure it is irrelevant.

But man's task is to make Christianity relevant in his own life. The principles are clear enough; the

266

teachings are there for man to accept or to reject. The actual relevance to a given situation is for each of us to make. Thomas More was beheaded for his moral conviction four hundred years ago. Thomas More saw the relevance of Christianity. He was, in his own words, the king's best servant, but God's first. And though he held an important political position, it was because he saw the relevance of Christianity in his life that he was canonized by the Church. Each of us can make—we must make—a similar decision in our own lives. Each of us can make Christianity relevant to our lives.

The physical death each of us shall undergo together with the rising after death must be preceded by a life that is dead to sin. By baptism we have been baptized into death, because by baptism we have been given a new life, the supernatural life of Christ within us. This new life, although completed in the next life after death, has actually begun in this life. By being alive to God now, by making Christ relevant now, we live for that moment when our lives are changed, the time when we shall leave this life and die.

But he said to them, 'There is no need for alarm.
You are looking for Jesus of Nazareth, who was crucified:
he has risen, he is not here. See, here is the place where
they laid him' [Mark 16:6].

RESURRECTION AND

TRIUMPHANT TRAGEDY

A MATCHBOOK COVER once attracted me because
on it was printed the insignia of a funeral home that
offered the accommodations of three chapels, air
conditioning, comfort, and ample parking space for
a delighted public. The cover's design suggested an
exclusive country club or an elegant restaurant, but
it was an advertisement for a dignified burial service.

It is curious, when you think of it, that death
should be treated in this manner. It is as if a man's
death were some great joke; yet we know that death

268

is no laughing matter. Here though is a man, a funeral director, driving a trade in death, displaying his mortuary with a salesman's smile as if he were advertising the pleasures of a luxury apartment.

Not only is this bit of Americana a joke, but it is also in the classic formula of comedy. For the comic writer lets loose the great forces of passion or of destiny only to show his characters responding to them with ludicrous triviality. The death joke, like sick humor or black comedy, cuts uncomfortably close to the bone, however, and almost breaks the comic formula. Because if someone dies, it is difficult to pretend that nothing of consequence has occurred.

Tragedy takes a path opposite from comedy. The full force of dangers threatening our comfort are disclosed in tragedy, and they are allowed their maximum effect. Lear drinks to the dregs the cup of his folly; Hamlet's experiment in just revenge makes a very bloody mess; no undeceiving circumstance turns Othello from the road of murderous jealousy.

Yet tragedy, while certainly more disturbing than comedy, is also more consoling than comedy. In comedy it is amusing, but not reassuring, to see the threats to our existence contrived or sidetracked into an anticlimax. In comedy we are left with the disquieting reflection that things might have turned out otherwise. Tragedy, for its part, refuses to load the dice in man's favor but permits him to see that even when the worst happens man can face it in some fashion or other.

One reason man can face this awful fact of the tragic, the ultimate expression of which is death, is that he accepts—perhaps, at times, unwittingly— the fact of the resurrection of the flesh assured to mankind by the historical Resurrection of Jesus. Because it was a triumph over death, Jesus' Resurrection is relevant to men at all times in history. In the light of the Resurrection, death can become for any man a triumphant tragedy.

We read today of the great need to elevate human life by providing food, shelter, recreation, health—in short, the good life for all mankind. Yet, hard as we may strive to reach this goal, it is humanly impossible. Fallen man is only too aware of the ineffectiveness of such universal providing. Neither the Russian system nor the American way of life—in fact, no economical system—brings a millenium. Man simply cannot satisfy all his needs and desires in this life by political or economic or military means alone.

The Resurrection clearly informs us that the millenium is not to be here, that man's ultimate desires are completed only beyond this life, that any hope of total fulfillment offered by the devices or systems of this world is an idolatry rooted in the belief that man has in his own power the capability of satisfying all his desires. Only a naïve humanism believes that man can so affect his condition in this life that he will achieve in this world perfect fulfillment and maximum happiness, that man has here his lasting city or his final destiny.

The Christian, therefore, is confronted with a deep and agonizing dilemma: the conflict between the obligations of this world, which are very real— the obligation, for instance, for the more affluent to provide for the less affluent, the need for sacrificing for the sake of one's neighbor—and his belief that man has not here a lasting city.

This dilemma is the Christian's occupational hazard. He may find himself with less enthusiasm for solving the world's problems than has the secular humanist. And yet the Christian betrays his calling if, in fighting this temptation, he contributes to the illusion that all there is to man's existence is the mission to feed the hungry and to clothe the naked. These are very important Christian virtues, indeed, but they hardly present the total picture of vital Christianity.

For some of the early Christians, everything was seen as having been accomplished with Jesus' Resurrection. Salvation was at hand. Only a short time remained, they thought, until the conclusion of this world. As time passed, however, some of Jesus' teaching about the growth and development of the kingdom began to dawn on them. They began to realize that the distance between the Resurrection and the second coming was certainly vast indeed. They began to comprehend the need to go out and to preach the good news of the Resurrection to all nations in all generations.

But the good news they preached about the resurrection of the flesh was a scandal to the Jewish community. It was foolishness to the Greeks. And yet it is the foundation of the Christian's belief.

For the resurrection of the flesh teaches man the limits and purposes of his political and cultural life, what he can expect and what he cannot expect from this world. The Resurrection teaches that man is mortal, that he must die, that he can expect what is humanly feasible in this world and no more. The Resurrection assures us that the elimination of hunger, of disease, of poverty cannot produce a man who will not in the end suffer and die.

Man's life is a tragedy; the Resurrection makes it a triumphant tragedy. The Resurrection teaches that man does in truth have desires beyond his temporal needs. And it is this very truth that exempts politics, economics, technology, and culture from making spurious demands and offering vain hopes that by themselves they can solve man's ultimate problems. For no single human doctrine can satisfactorily solve the question of man's essence and man's destiny. That question is theological, and the foundation of that theology is the resurrection of the flesh —the belief that, if faithful to the demands of charity and justice in this life, man will one day rise.

Thus the Christian stands as testimony before the world that salvation lies not in this life, but rather is achieved through this life. And since it is achieved only through this life, the tasks of this world are definitely Christian tasks. The Christian, though, bears witness that the tasks of this world are not the ultimate goal, nor the sole purpose of his existence.

The resurrection of the flesh, as prefigured in the Resurrection of Jesus, is a most contemporary dogma, most relevant to man's practical situation. Behind welfare and security and the good life lies the resurrection of the flesh. Who promises man more, betrays man.

The first and final freedom of the Christian is precisely this freedom to affirm that our world is inadequate. Whoever believes that this world is sufficient or can be made sufficient through human effort diminishes man. He who accepts the Resurrection sees both worlds for what they are, and this viewing of both worlds realistically is what the resurrection of the flesh means for us today; it is what it signified yesterday and will signify tomorrow and forever.

Now if Christ raised from the dead is what
has been preached, how can some of you be saying
that there is no resurrection of the dead?
If there is no resurrection of the dead,
Christ himself cannot have been raised,
and if Christ has not been raised
then our preaching is useless and
your believing it is useless [1 Corinthians 15:12-14].

LIFT UP YOUR HEARTS

ST. PAUL SO insists on the efficacy and the significance of Jesus' Resurrection that he may well bore
sane Christians with his frequent repetitions of that
event's importance. Any boredom, though, seems
less the fault of Paul's rhetoric than of the tendency
among many American Catholics to be neither play-
ful nor joyful in their service of God. And the Resurrection, whatever else it may be, is a cause for
Christians to rejoice.

Today, especially, gaiety seldom appears among
our prophets of doom, among our unhappy clergy,

274

our harassed hierarchy, and our disgruntled laity. One would think that Jesus had failed to rise from the dead and so assure Christians of their ultimate happiness.

Our American culture imbued with puritanical Calvinism may explain, but it hardly justifies, the prevalent Jansenism that exists among Catholics. Paul's words on the Resurrection support our response at Mass when, to the invitation "Lift up your hearts," we joyfully respond, "We have lifted them up to the Lord." The question is: Have we? In England, they say, things are always serious, but never desperate, whereas in Ireland things are always desperate, but never serious. The Resurrection of Jesus Christ should prompt among us a more Irish than English attitude. So let us ask ourselves quite seriously: Have I really lifted up my heart to God?

The Resurrection's relevancy is related to the very basis of Christian faith. St. Paul declares that without the Resurrection Christianity is a cipher, and all preaching is useless and vain. Certainly, as we read the accounts of the Resurrection in the Scriptures one fact stands forth as eminently clear: the early Christians were convinced that Jesus who was crucified rose from the dead, thus assuring Christians of a life that would conquer death and sin.

Christians may consider the Resurrection as a great proof for the divinity of Jesus, which it is; the Resurrection is his greatest sign. Christians may consider the Resurrection as the final completion of the redemptive act, which it is; the Resurrection remains forever linked with Christ's passion and death. Christians may consider the Resurrection as that event whereby we are assured one day of rising successfully to our final goal, finding at last unending happiness and undying love. The Resurrection of Jesus is all these. So the relevancy of the Resurrection to Christianity is fully apparent; it is the veritable source of the Christian's belief.

The idea of resurrection, of course, was not completely new to the time of Christ. There was a hint at resurrection for man in the Old Testament, and ancient pagan writers often spoke of a metempsychosis by which a man's soul would return to this world after death in another body. Such beliefs simply highlight man's indomitable desire to live, to be immortal. Faced with the awful transiency of this life, man painfully attempted to discover some further existence after death. The Resurrection of Jesus assures the Christian that his search has ended.

Now the relevancy of the Resurrection should lead a Christian first of all to a proper evaluation of death. It is death that leads to resurrection for every man as for Jesus. Yet there is a tendency for some dour Christians to consider death solely as a separation, as a loss, as a very grim situation. Nothing, of course, can totally eliminate the human sorrow naturally felt by those whom the deceased person leaves behind. But death should remind a Christian of his ultimate happiness, because death leads to a fuller life now that Jesus has risen. Because of the Resurrection, death should no longer be simply a grim admonition that our time approaches and we had better be prepared, but a reminder of our very goal. In a sense, death and resurrection are one and the same.

Besides suggesting an appropriate attitude toward death, prayerful consideration of the Resurrection will also lead the Christian to a realistic appraisal of life itself. The Christian must resemble neither the optimist who believes that this world is the best of all possible worlds nor the pessimist who is afraid that this world is the best of all possible worlds. The Christian is a realist who sees this world for what it is: a means, not an end; a process, not a product. And the Christian who accepts the teaching of the Resurrection properly and considers its true significance will not be conned, either, by secular humanists and agnostics who attempt to persuade him that this world is a lasting city, who urge him to become involved solely with this life.

Prayerful consideration of the Resurrection, finally, enables a Christian to build his spiritual life; it enables him to anticipate the future happily and hopefully. Too often in our spiritual lives we are like people who are constantly clearing away debris but never building. For too many Christians continue to prepare the site for their spiritual edifice, when they ought to get on with the actual construction. Too many Christians sustain a sixth-grader's attitude toward their faith, seeing it only as a system of rules and laws, willing to rely on simplistic notions, and fearful of growing in that happiness which is the Christian's portion in this life precisely because of the Resurrection.

Admittedly we Christians are sinners, but Christ has conquered sin and death for us. It is our task to join ourselves to him so that we live in him, with him, and through him. Yet some very sincere Christians constantly torture themselves with remorse and fear of past sins. They seemingly delight in morbid thoughts of a wrathful, punishing God. All too seldom, if ever, does this type of Christian look outward beyond his own sinfulness to discover the God of charity, the God who promises life, the God who supports his pledge with the reassuring Resurrection of Jesus Christ.

Man must work positively at building his spiritual life, not just at clearing the ground. Devout Christians inclined toward the morbid and gruesome must cease flagellating themselves with fear and remorse and look directly at the risen Jesus. Many of them act as if they are about to be condemned to an eternity in some Dantesque inferno; they seem unaware of the joy that should accompany the Christian through life. They have orally answered the invitation, "Lift up your hearts," but they haven't really responded from the depths of their souls. I am not suggesting spiritual complacency or presumption, but I am suggesting a realistic appraisal of true Christian response in the light of the Resurrection of Jesus.

Now the Christian observes the relevance of the Resurrection of Jesus only if he understands the faith and the mystery that is the substance of Christianity. Too often a Christian wants to see absolutely clearly in a rationalistic way, to know exactly on which side the slice of bread is buttered. And this attitude conditions his practice of his faith. He uses the confessional to get him off the hook, not as a place in which to meet Christ in a sacrament of love. He attends Mass, passively fulfilling an obligation, but he fails to assist fully at Mass, he forgets even to acknowledge at Mass the God who loves him. He approaches a priest as if that priest were his conscience, forgetting that no man can abdicate to any other man his duty of settling matters of conscience for himself.

This type of Christian overlooks the obvious fact that Christianity is revelation, not philosophy. He overlooks the fact that man does not see clearly in revelation, but only, as Paul himself says, darkly. If the Christian knows the slice of bread is buttered, why must he worry about which side the butter is on? Doesn't he eat both sides of the bread at the same time? The genuine Christian takes Christianity and the Resurrection for what they are, without demanding added rationalizations to convince him.

The Resurrection of Jesus gives a greater unity, a fuller significance, a deeper reason, and a staunch promise to the Christian's life. The poet Yeats sought to bring order into the chaos he witnessed around him, a chaos that still confronts each of us who is even slightly aware of life and its involvements. Poor old Yeats developed an involved system of his own for coping, because he couldn't accept traditional Christianity. Yet the Resurrection of Jesus is surely sufficient for ordering the confusion in our minds, if only we give ourselves wholeheartedly to belief in it and live in the joyful spirit that the Resurrection should prompt in a Christian soul even in a joyless age.

Ironically, Yeats even at the end of his life was unsatisfied with his system; he could do no more than exclaim that perhaps he would wither into the truth. But the true Christian might have told Yeats his system was doomed from the start, for Yeats tried to square the circle: he attempted to rationalize revelation and the spiritual life when only a personal acceptance of mystery can fully satisfy the longing of man's heart or the Christian in his faith.

Paul in his preaching emphasizes the Resurrection of Jesus for the very reason that Jesus rose from the dead, namely, to reinforce his claim and to support the promise of Christianity. Unlike Marxism and humanistic agnosticism, which promise a total satisfaction in this world here and now, Christianity is constructed upon fidelity to the God-Man and to his cause in the hope that one day man will find his ultimate fulfillment. This day, the day of our death, is the day of our own resurrection, which is assured us by Jesus' own rising from the dead. At every offering of the sacrifice of the Mass we are indeed invited to lift up our hearts. The Christian response must ever be, as it is in the liturgy, "We have lifted them up to the Lord."

About this book

And Now a Word from Our Creator was set in the composing room of Loyola University Press. The typeface is 12/15 Caledonia and the display type is 12 Caledonia.

It was printed by Photopress, Inc., on Warren's 60-pound English Finish paper and bound by The Engdahl Company.